PRAISE FOR *COLOR TODAY PRETTY*

"This little book is a big inspiration! If you've forgotten how blessed you are, Stephanie will remind you. If you've lost track of the beauty of the moment, Stephanie will shine the light on it, and if you've forgotten how pretty the day is, Stephanie will awaken you with a story about it. Her authenticity, warmth and wisdom shine through each page of this encouraging tome! Don't waste a minute. Pick up this book immediately and Color Today Pretty!"

Elizabeth Jeffries
Author, *What Exceptional Executives Need to Know*

"This book streamlines the necessity of making the most out of this treasure we have been given called life and, more importantly, teaches us to look through the lens of vulnerability and purpose to see what this life is all about. Our ability to escape the tragedies of life's distractions is a gift within itself and we are drawn to so much more when we 'choose' to make life happen instead of letting life happen to us. So in order to *color today pretty,* we have to let our dreams flow instead of keeping them locked up in the box of fear, and allow our God inhabit the dreams He gave us so that they manifest into a more meaningful and beautiful reality."

Devin E. West, M. Div.
Senior Leader, First Trinity Baptist Church, Jeffersonville

“Most of us move too quickly through life to notice just how special each moment, each memory and each person can be to our own existence. Stephanie calls us all to stop and realize that, with our own brush strokes and perspectives in our own lives, we *can* color today pretty.”

Dawne Gee
News Anchor, Raycom Media

“YOU have the choice to choose your perspective! Stephanie has written a very colorful book that reminds us that God gives us choices daily to see His divine plan in our lives. She shows us that these small moments can end up having the biggest impact upon our lives. May this book awaken the souls of all who are privileged to lay their eyes on every page, right to the very end.”

Damien K. H. Nash, aka Coach Nash
Award-winning Certified Life Coach, Top Selling Author of *#CompletelySingle*, Founder of Completely You 365, LLC.

“Stephanie’s ability to see God working in her life through ordinary moments is truly inspiring. If you are looking to find everyday miracles and peace in your life, you will love reading this book!”

Cheryl Ann Silich
American Gladiators Champion and
Community Link Christian Radio Show Host

“In her incredible new book, *Color Today Pretty*, Stephanie Feger shows you the power of perspective and the tools you need to change your perspective on life. By sharing her own personal struggles and successes, Stephanie opens your eyes to the extraordinary events of day-to-day life and teaches you that every day is, indeed, extraordinary.”

Mark D. Rucker
Speaker and Author of *Unleash the Beast*

"Stephanie Feger's book, *Color Today Pretty*, is a breath of fresh air! Stephanie is out to find the sacred in the secular and the holy in the humdrum. As she shares vignettes from her life, you realize that it is possible to experience life in a new and rewarding way. Highly recommended!"

Cathy Fyock
The Business Book Strategist and Author

"I just finished reading Stephanie's book. Wow — it's life-changing for me! I now know that living a life in perspective really isn't as hard as I sometimes think it is and it's so worth it."

Steve Vest
Editor and Publisher, *Kentucky Monthly* magazine

"Life is not always easy. Things don't always go as planned. Even in our most difficult and challenging moments, we have a choice. How we roll with the ups and downs of the everyday is a matter of the perspective we choose. In *Color Today Pretty*, Stephanie Feger gives us a Spirit-filled guidebook to making the choices that lead to a life well-lived, a life of purpose and contentment."

Michael Holtz
Author of *It's Not Harder Than Cancer*

"I've been passionate about perspective for more than a decade, as the power of perspective and gratitude completely changed the experience my daughter and I shared through her leukemia journey. It is fun to witness others experiencing similar awareness, as they choose to challenge their perspectives. *Color Today Pretty* is a sweet invitation to see life through a different lens. This opportunity is something each of us can easily embrace and be blessed by."

Denise Taylor
Speaker, Author of *Heavenly Birth: A Mother's Journey, A Daughter's Legacy*

"Stephanie Feger's book is a living example of listening to the spirit when it calls us to live our purpose. As you read *Color Today Pretty,* you will be encouraged, inspired and moved to connect to the Creator's spirit that is innately inside of YOU. Stephanie's personal story will open your mind to finding your unique purpose in being the change you want to see in the world."

Tasha Wahl
Founder of The Butterfly Effect

"*Color Today Pretty* is this little gem of a book from a dear friend that isn't a one-and-done read. This book has a simple yet powerful message that should be read DAILY: YOU get to choose the lens through which YOU view life. Choose to color today pretty. Choose to read this extremely relatable story often as a reminder that life is what you make it."

Kelly K
Radio Personality, Louisville, Kentucky

"I've known Stephanie Feger for many years and have always supported her both personally and professionally. I admire how she speaks from her heart and soul and now we get to read about her experiences that are filled with conviction and honesty. I'm looking forward to taking Stephanie up on her challenge to us all … are YOU?"

Tammy McNeill
Broadcast Producer

"*Color Today Pretty* offers the reader an opportunity to enter into the wonderful, colorful life of the author, her husband, her children and her faith-family. These litanies of blessings in ordinary life experiences are as entertaining as they are insightful of God's grace at work. Earthly life events are logged here, and almost everyone would find common ground in how God amazes us. I recommend this vivid, honest and genuinely written book to everyone who savors life as it unfolds day to day. It is wonderfully written and divinely inspired!"

Father Dale Cieslik
Pastor, St. Francis Xavier Catholic Church, Mt. Washington, KY;
Archivist, Roman Catholic Archdiocese of Louisville

"Stephanie powerfully describes events that typify those of many young women but does so with the wise reflections of maturity. Her words bring hope and strength to others, enabling them to claim their own power and strength and to move through and beyond those things that might otherwise hold them back."

Michael Johnson
President, Mercy Academy

"Working with Stephanie Feger always leaves me energized because her perspective on life is contagious. She constantly shows me that even amidst challenges life deals us, there is still good in this world."

Nate Butler
Executive Vice President of Operations,
Orbital Media Networks Inc, Denver, Colorado

"Through some of the highest peaks of life and the deepest valleys, Stephanie's beautiful spirit is driven by her deep relationship with God and family to be authentic in everyday life. A must-read book!"

Peggy Wolf, APRN
OB/GYN Nurse Practitioner, Women First of Louisville

"Love it!!!! This gal is AMAZE-ing … meaning she looks at life with amazement. She sees everything brand new. She is a MERCY WOMAN, one who lives and breathes the Corporal and Spiritual works of Mercy. Use this book as a tool for your own journey. She's "pretty" right in target!"

Karen D. Kuenzig
Music Director, Retreat Director, Spiritual Director,
Spiritually Religious Woman

"My thanks to Stephanie for sharing her thoughts and feelings with us in this new book. Her words are very moving, powerful and inspiring. As a 23-year cancer survivor, I found that her words are able to express many of the thoughts and feelings I continue to harbor. We often times do not know the effect our words and actions have on others. Saying 'God Bless You' can be all someone who is really struggling might need to make it through the day. We all need to have a mission in life, and Stephanie has helped provide some ideas for her readers about finding that purpose. Unlike no other of God's creations, we have been given the power of CHOICE. That also means that we can choose to, or, not to, do something. We just have to remember that 'We are blessed to be a blessing to others.'"

John Huggins
Retired Educator

"I met Stephanie on an 'ordinary' Saturday in an 'ordinary' church building, but what has come to fruition since I met her has convinced me that the thesis of her book is correct. God is in the ordinary working overtime to show us he loves us. Stephanie's mission is to spread this awareness with her work. I am truly grateful that our paths crossed like they did."

Elizabeth Johnson
Educator

COLOR TODAY PRETTY

An Inspirational Guide to Living a Life in Perspective

STEPHANIE FEGER

Color Today Pretty: An Inspirational Guide to Living a Life in Perspective

Published by Silver Tree Publishing, a division of Silver Tree Communications, LLC (Kenosha, WI).
www.SilverTreeCommunications.com

Editing by:
Hilary Jastram
Eric Walker
Kate Colbert

Cover design by:
Mattie Naylor

Typesetting by:
Courtney Hudson

First edition, May 2018

ISBN: 978-0-9990612-2-0

Library of Congress Control Number: 2018939391

Created in the United States of America

TABLE OF CONTENTS

Dedication 1

Introduction 3

Prelude 7

Always by Your Side 9

1: Having Faith 11
2: The Wait 17
3: The Perfect Fall 23
4: You're Never Lost 27
5: Nothing is by Chance 33

Ordinary Miracles 39

6: No, Thank You 41
7: You Will Never Be Hungry 45
8: Walking Angels 49
9: Be the Bow 53
10: The Redbird 57

Perfect Imperfection **61**

11: Do Your Best 63

12: You Get to Choose 67

13: Making Memories 73

14: I See You 77

15: Broken Beautiful 81

Live Life Childlike **87**

16: The Present 89

17: We're More Alike 93

18: It's All About the Play-Doh 97

19: The Essence of Magic 101

20: Be the Reason 107

The Power of One **113**

21: Your Story Matters 115

22: A Good Deed Doesn't Go Unnoticed 119

23: Best Friends 125

24: Finding Angels 129

25: Believe in Humanity 135

Be Love 139

26: Love Her Heart 141

27: The Couple 145

28: Together 151

29: I Love You, Too, Momma 157

30: A Garden of Love 161

The Journey 167

31: Cherish Today 169

32: My Life. Period. 175

33: My Last Day 181

34: Get Me 187

35: Dream On 193

Conclusion 197

Acknowledgments 203

About the Author 207

Learn More 209

DEDICATION

This book is dedicated to those who believe in others who may not believe in themselves. To those who help build confidence and encourage others to find their voice, no matter how hard it is to find. To those who have a story that needs to be heard but who may be too scared to share. To the lives that are touched by those doing good in this world in a way that may never be known.

To each of you, this book is dedicated to your continued perseverance, your abundant compassion and your consistent kindness. May more stories be told, more voices be found and more faith instilled as together we all learn to live a life in perspective.

INTRODUCTION

AN ORDINARY GIRL, LIVING LIFE EXTRAORDINARILY

My life really isn't extraordinary or special ... at least not in the sense that most people would think. I don't own a mansion or always wear the hot name-brand clothing line, and I can't afford to shop at only local, organic stores.

No. My life isn't extraordinary in the material sense.

But, today I woke up. My husband and I attended to our typical wild mornings getting the kids ready for school, but amidst the craziness, we took a moment to stare at the fading stars in the day's landscape while I hugged each one before they left. My eyes, while not perfect, took in God's beauty. My nails may not be freshly manicured; however, I am grateful that I have two hands to type this and two feet to walk anywhere I want. My belly is always full, and I have clothes on my back.

You see, I'm just a simple girl with a husband, three feisty "young'uns," and a cat as her sidekick. Nothing makes me stand out from you in a crowd except maybe my loud voice which God did bless me with the vigor to use.

Speaking of God, He's my rock, but I'd be lying if I didn't admit that some days I forget to lean on Him. On those days, I tend to get consumed with the things many of us do; distractors that eat up our time but give us nothing back in return. During those days, if I can pry myself away from a computer screen, I realize that while I may not be leaning on Him, He's never left. He's patiently waiting for me to realize the essence of what can make life meaningful. What makes you and me meaningful. And it all comes down to choice.

You have the choice. Each day you're faced with it.

Each moment, it's there. You may not get a say in how your day is going to go, but you get to choose the lens through which you experience and process it. You get to choose your attitude and your actions to what the world around you serves. You get to choose which version of yourself you'd like to be. Which YOU are you today at this very moment?

Life, you see, is about perspective. It's about opening our eyes to the world beyond superficial items and the digital and social worlds we are addicted to — myself included. It's about soaking in the moments around us; it's about *making moments* quite frankly or at least making time for moments to be made. I've learned that when you close your eyes and open your heart, God places some pretty remarkable moments in your life. This book is a collection of my moments.

While I may not be rich in the ways we all dream, I am rich in perspective, and to me, that is worth more than anything money can buy.

I hope that as you get a snapshot into some of my personal moments, you can chisel away at all the stuff in your life holding you back from fully being present in your moment. Because it's when that moment happens, that you can see the true miracles all around you. I promise they are everywhere.

PRELUDE

I had a dream many years ago. I was in a busy room with people auditioning to be the next "big star," and as the judge, I stood between a person's dream and their reality. I got to make the final call.

A young boy came to the stage to share his talent, which I had deemed subpar. I gave him the news that he wouldn't go any further in the competition. This was the end of the road.

Instead of harboring anger when he received the news, he wore a smile as he approached me holding out his hand. He gave me a picture he drew, and while I don't remember just what was on the page, I do recall what he said. He looked me in the eyes and spoke: "Color something pretty today!"

Most of my dreams linger for only a short time before my brain replaces them with schedules of chores or parenting duties. But this dream stuck with me all day.

At first, I was frustrated with myself for not letting this kid accomplish his dreams. *Why had I been so brash and rude?* Then this boy, who should have been livid at me, was joyful and actually gave *me* a present.

It hit me hours later. The dream had meaning much deeper than I saw on the surface and it was what the young boy said, not what he did, that mattered. *Color something pretty today.* He had a choice. He may not have been able to choose his outcome in the competition, but he chose his reaction to it. He shared that with me while he left me with the challenge to do the same, to color pretty things — to be positive and do good for one another. He wanted me to see the world through the lens of love instead of judgment and help him color this world something amazing. And he wanted me to start today.

You're thinking I'm a crazy, right? One dream and I've analyzed it to such a level that it doesn't make sense. Well, I promise you that dream was a challenge from our Higher Being, and He expects me to take up the task daily. These messages are in your life, too. If you pause and reflect on things that have happened, people you've come across, places you've been and experiences you've encountered … you will see them. If you really look at your life, you will see these messages everywhere!

Sometimes these messages smack you right in the face, but nine times out of 10 they are subtler. You have to be open to seeing them. You have to have the right lens on when you're viewing your life. This young boy pushed me to be a better me and inspire others to do the same. Many times, I stumble, not wanting to see the silver lining in my most painful experiences, but I'm trying. Isn't that what life is about? Trying?

No one said you had to be perfect. No, you don't even have to color your picture within the lines. You'll make plenty of mistakes and wrong turns. I know I have and I will. But each day is a new day, and each day I'll try my hardest to color that day pretty. I'm up for the challenge. *Are you?*

SECTION 1

ALWAYS BY YOUR SIDE

No matter how alone you feel, you never are. Even when there is no one in sight, sometimes that is when He is the most present. Close your eyes and have faith. Believe. Trust. Know that in your brightest of days and darkest of nights, He is always with you. He has never left your side; not for one moment.

Having Faith

The Wait

The Perfect Fall

You're Never Lost

Nothing is by Chance

CHAPTER 1
Having Faith

I've always wanted to be a mom. There was a place deep within my heart where I knew nothing in this world would complete me until I got to hold a baby in my arms and learn firsthand what it means to experience selfless love. I prayed for years about it, even before I met my husband.

My husband had the same wish. So, once we settled in a house large enough to hold all the stuff that comes with a baby, we felt it was time. But as the months went by, our bathroom garbage can filled with ovulation strips and failed pregnancy tests. The worry sank in as I began to question if I would ever be a mother. Then the dream came.

Only a few short months after my wedding, my grandma had lost her battle with cancer. While cancer stole a lot from her, nothing could steal her unwavering faith and beautiful spirit. Nothing, no matter how hard it tried.

A day never goes by that I don't think of her, and my heartache goes deep. She was my family's sounding board; the lady who loved me no matter what and always called me "Sugs." When she told me everything would be alright, I believed her. During this time when something I wanted so bad felt so out of reach, I wanted nothing more than for her to tell me that all I needed to do was trust in God's plan.

I may not have been able to call her on the phone to get that satisfaction, but a few nights before Christmas that year she came to me in a dream. She was as beautiful as before. Her hair vivid red; her gaze direct; and her smile so sincere. I didn't hear her southern drawl, and "Sug" didn't slip out, but it didn't matter. She exuded a peaceful and joyous demeanor that calmed my weary soul.

She approached me as if she didn't need her feet to walk, and as she handed me a folded piece of paper, I could feel the endless love she had always had for me. She smiled as I opened the note that she secretly had delivered. The message was short, but the impact nearly robbed me of my breath. It read:

"Great-Grandma can't wait to meet your little one."

It was as if my heart stopped as I knew immediately the news that she was chosen to deliver. No, an impersonal pregnancy test was not going to be how I found out about this miracle. Instead, I got a direct message from heaven.

Then I awoke.

While God had already hand delivered the news, a positive pregnancy test on Christmas Eve proved that our prayers were answered. We were going to be parents.

While enjoyable, movies unfortunately help to create a false sense of reality. Like when you find your true love, beautiful music doesn't linger in the wind. And one thing is for certain; a pregnancy doesn't always lead to swollen feet and water puddles. In fact, some women never even make it to that stage.

I was all smiles until the weekend. Then it was the worst weekend I have had to date as the bleeding started. After trying to be strong, on Monday, I begged my doctor for a follow-up ultrasound. I was so worried. You see, even though I was merely weeks pregnant, I had already begun to venture into the deep depths of love that only a parent can understand. As uncertain I may have been, when I heard the radio personality on my alarm clock that morning, I was reminded that no matter what, everything would be alright.

"For those of you out there that are having a tough time, know that God is with you. No matter the trial or tribulation, God is by your side. You see, God can make the impossible, possible." As had happened with the dream, God had strategically placed another message into my life, this one speaking directly to me.

An ultrasound identified a hematoma which was likely the culprit for the bleeding, so for a moment, I could breathe a little better, relishing in the fact that I got to see the baby's heartbeat that day. While it wasn't ideal, the doctor wasn't worried. Yet.

The next day proved to be worse than before, and another ultrasound brought with it tears instead of smiles. In less than 24 hours, my baby became unattached to my uterine wall and had no way of receiving what she needed from me to thrive. No matter how hard I wanted to help her, there was nothing I could do but watch her struggle, knowing that each heartbeat was one closer to her last.

The doctor confirmed that we were on the verge of losing her, but she knew that my faith was too strong to give up as I hoped for a miracle. Even when the bleeding worsened and the pain drew me to my knees, I couldn't accept what was happening. My heart didn't want to believe what my head knew was truth, even when I approached the moment where I knew with one toilet flush, I had probably lost the one treasure that I cared the most for.

Those several days when I could barely walk, all I was left to do was think. I laid on the couch screaming to God about all my frustrations with the situation He had put me in. Why would He give me a glimpse into a new world of amazement to then steal my joy? I was so mad, and rightfully so.

Just as I was digging myself into the depths of depression, the phone rang. It was my aunt who begged to talk to me. I didn't have the strength to talk to anyone, but I obliged. In between sobs, I listened to what she told me. She, too, had experienced a miscarriage, and it was just as traumatic to her soul as it was proving to be to mine. But what she shared with me that night was exactly what my heart needed to hear.

As she recounted my dream, she pushed me to take a step back and listen, really listen, to the message my grandma had delivered. "Great-Grandma can't wait to meet your little one." Upon original receipt of that message, I was delighted, knowing that my grandma was thrilled that we would be blessed with a baby. But now, only after my aunt pleaded with me to really hear the message, I realized what it had meant all along.

I wasn't meant to ever hold this baby, at least not in this world. She wasn't meant to be the sparkle in our eyes as we watched her grow. I wasn't going to see her find the love of her life or have a baby of her own. No, that was never the intent of her life. Instead, she was meant to brighten my grandma's days; my grandma, the woman who was always taking care of others, had someone to take care of now. I wasn't going to get to hold this baby, but my grandma was going to. I wasn't going to get to experience the joy I knew this sweet baby would bring us, but my grandma would get to soak up every ounce of her beauty as they would wait together until the day our family would be reunited.

The message was so clear. Great-Grandma couldn't wait to meet my baby, and the moment that her heart fluttered its last beat I am confident that my grandma's hand was outstretched, smiling as she brought her home. There I was, so angry at God for what He had done to me that I didn't realize what He had done for my grandma. It was at that moment that I realized I had a critical choice to make. I would grieve my loss and then, like my baby, put out my hand at the moment I had no energy left and realize that my only way through anything would be with Him by my side.

That moment, when I felt no ounce of my life was worth living, I put out my hand to let Him take over. Making that choice was not easy, but I promise you that it was the best decision I ever made.

A day doesn't go by that I don't think about her. Faith that is. That's what I named her the moment I realized that while her life was short-lived here, she taught me what true faith is all about. It's only now, years later, that I can see when I felt like I was at my end, it was only my beginning.

Having faith means so much more when you've been on the brink of not having it. Your life may feel empty as it fills with pain, but it's at that moment when you need faith the most. You realize that control isn't something you own, but He does. And in a moment, the pain that you feel can be exchanged for comfort. All you have to do is stretch out your hand and let Him take over.

I know that one day, my family will be reunited. Until then, Faith made room in my heart for a love that is indescribable, and her purpose wasn't complete until Great-Grandma got to meet her. Her life will never be for not because while I may have lost my Faith, because of her, I will never lose faith.

CHAPTER 2

The Wait

I hadn't felt like myself for months as a nasty stomach bug had thrown me to the curb. I had thought I would wake up one morning and bounce back, but after so long feeling off I started to forget what normal felt like.

I called my doctor in hopes to get to the bottom of it, but that conversation proved to be more frustrating than the lingering illness itself. The receptionist noted that they would be happy to get me in … in two weeks. And if waiting that long wasn't an option, she shared that office protocol encouraged me to take myself to the nearest immediate care center instead.

Even though my to-do list was already long, I decided that finding a new doctor needed to be added to it. Thank goodness for friends because a dear one recommended her relative who happened to be a practicing physician in my small town. By coincidence or fate, he was accepting new patients! I felt I could check that worry off the list. Or so I thought.

This doctor was much more thorough than I planned for, and he didn't take anything at face-value. What a welcome change. When he heard wheezing in my lungs, he immediately ordered an X-ray, determined to get to the bottom of whatever it was.

You know the feeling you get when someone you meet earns your trust the instant they speak. It's like you've known them for years as if they are extensions of your own family — a family that cares deeply for every ounce of you. We are called to be connected like this, yet it seems this ability is the exception, not the rule nowadays. But this doctor exemplified every bit of that quality the moment I met him, and I knew immediately when he called for additional tests, I would do them, no questions asked.

I waited in the room for the doctor to return, expecting him to inform me that the picture looked clean and to wish me well until we met again. Instead, he came in accompanied by his nurse and promptly shut the door. He noted he had an embarrassing question to ask, and I giggled to myself knowing that the word "embarrassing" was no longer compatible with my body. After having three kids, I had left all my modesty at home. He showed me the area of his concern on my chest X-ray and wanted further testing done on my breast to better understand what we could potentially be up against.

I held it together. Smiled like we all do even when we hear things we don't want to and put on a façade that apparently wasn't thick enough as I cracked later when sharing the news with my family. I had so many questions running in my head. You know the ones where you try to rationalize why you? Instead of why not you? I was young and felt like this worry shouldn't be mine. While a large part of me believed that nothing was wrong, a small part doubted. While I believed that no matter what happened God would help me through it, but like it does many times in our lives, worry set in and clouded my positive perspective.

So, the wait began. The wait for the doctor's office to place the orders for my follow-up tests. The wait for my OBGYN to find availability to see me. Challenges appeared at every turn. No appointment spot for a month. No digital X-ray to forward to my other doctors. I fought until I felt like there wasn't any fight left in me just to get what I needed to hopefully ease my mind. But none of it came fast, and I felt like I was counting time using one grain of sand at a time.

I'd become accustomed to waiting. During one of my pregnancies a few years prior, I had gotten a healthy dose of it. At that time, I had gone in for an ultrasound, not of my breast but of my belly, to get a glimpse of our family's newest addition. As any parent will tell you, the experience is supposed to be a joyous occasion, seeing your baby growing appropriately and hearing their strong heartbeat echo off the cramped room's walls. But, as someone who had experienced loss before, those appointments always came with a cocktail of anxiety and a splash of trepidation. That day was no different.

I saw a growing baby, who looked so protected, and yet I could tell that the ultrasound tech was mustering up the courage to give me troubling news. I knew through the panic in her eyes that she was worried. She was searching for a heartbeat and couldn't understand why that proved difficult.

We heard it, and then we didn't. It was intermittent and inconsistent, but it was there. This sweet little baby was trying but wasn't living up to the standards expected of it. The ultrasound tech stopped trying, and with a hug and some tears, wished me luck.

Even though the tests may have proved otherwise, something in my heart told me to hold strong, pray and not give up. My doctor, while holding my hand, tried to be real without robbing me of hope. She, too, had been in these predicaments before, with the outcome of the pendulum swinging either way. All we could do was wait and repeat the ultrasound again in a few days to determine my sweet baby's fate. I wept, and my doctor did, too. The wait began.

I've never been patient, and I venture to say that I'm not the only one who wants it, and wants it now. If you can't get it for me, I'll do so myself. However, just place someone in a position where you can't press the fast-forward button, and you'll realize there are many events that happen far beyond our control.

Both of these instances required me to give up any belief that I could conquer this alone and admit that I needed Him. I needed God to hold my hand, to literally carry me as my legs wanted to give out and my spirit wanted to give up. I had to believe that while I couldn't take care of the situations, that didn't mean they weren't being taken care of.

That's the essence of faith, isn't it? Believing what you don't visibly see. Knowing what you feel in your heart is real and true. Following even when you don't know where the road will take you. It's not blindly following or living a life of naivety; it's much more than that. It's trusting in a way that you never knew possible. When you literally have no other choice, what else can you do but trust?

My patience has been tested to the brink many times, but these two occurrences made everything else look trivial. I got through it, step-by-step, moment-by-moment, breath-by-breath. Sometimes, that is the only way. And when the wait concluded, the walk into the doctor's office felt like the conclusion of running a marathon. That feeling where you are at that point of exhaustion yet thrilled to finally reach the finish line.

I could see in the eyes of the ultrasound tech that day as she read my chart that she knew the follow-up ultrasound was a make-or-break moment for my baby. The mammogram tech, too, prayed that she could give me the news this girl yearned to hear. As nervous as I was in both instances, I'm sure both of them were as well. And each of those days positive results were delivered. The heartbeat was there, and consistent, and loud! There was no question that this sweet baby was here to stay. The mammogram was clear; not a concern to even think about. Both outcomes were well worth the wait. Hope prevailed.

I know not every wait concludes with happy tears and joyous hugs. I realize that these instances could have ended quite differently, and I was prepared for it to the best extent I could be. The wait gave me that. It gave me time to find meaning and purpose. It gave me time to find peace. It gave me time to find God.

I'm still not patient. I don't know if I ever will be. I'm sure that there will be a day where the conclusion of my wait won't end on a positive note. But I realize now more than ever that things aren't supposed to happen in my time, but rather in His.

Don't give up. Don't become impatient. Try hard not to worry. A marathoner's step over the finish line wouldn't be so victorious if it didn't come with the strenuous run prior; your wait is extremely purposeful and beyond worth it. I promise.

CHAPTER 3
The Perfect Fall

We've always been ritualistic church attenders. Yes, we may be late, but we are there. This particular Sunday concluded the annual church picnic, which meant that not only would mass itself be overflowing, but two-thirds of the parking lot would be home to numerous tent structures. Not a good combination for a family with young kids who were inevitably never early.

Thirty-two weeks pregnant, I drove our SUV to where it teetered on the grassy hill and pavement turned make-shift parking spot that would have to do for the time being. My husband got our oldest kid out of the car, and I unstrapped my daughter from her seat and she promptly latched to my side since my basketball belly was clearly in the way. We proceeded to make our way into the church. Except, I never made it.

The unfortunate place I had opted to park mixed with a dress that was too long was a recipe for disaster. I tripped. I stumbled. I fell. No matter the length of time since this event has occurred, the sequence of events is imprinted in my mind, and while the event itself was tragic enough, what I remember most vividly was watching my baby girl fly out of my arms.

My husband rushed over as I yelled for him to grab our daughter. I was immobilized from shock, but my legs were also contorted in such a way that I didn't know how to unravel them to help her. I still had hold of her legs, but from my view, I was sure that when he would pick her up, I would see a scene from a horror flick.

He grabbed our daughter and proceeded to ask about me. I didn't care about me. I couldn't feel me. All I could feel was the ache in my stomach that I wasn't able to protect my daughter from pain. She was screaming from the deep depths of her lungs, but somehow not a scratch was found on her face.

I didn't allow the sobs to come until the moment that I released her legs after I knew she was safe in my husband's arms. I kept asking him to look her over — something had happened to her; I knew it. Yet, everywhere he looked, all he found was blemish-free baby skin.

Me, on the other hand … When I fell, I landed on my left leg with my calf and foot underneath me. My right leg was bent in a weird position and too was propping up my body. The next day I would feel the full aftermath of the incident; however, nothing would compare to the ache I felt in my heart.

As a parent, nothing matters more than the health, safety and happiness of one's children. Not only do I pray for those three things each night, I also feel it is my duty to do everything possible to help make that a reality for each of them, from carrying them in my belly to holding their hands through life.

That Sunday, I felt like I let down my two youngest. But the story I continued to tell myself and the story that really happened weren't the same.

Life is all about perspective. Seeing something from one angle may not provide you the full truth. Sometimes you have to take a step back and look from multiple positions to understand really what is unfolding in front of you.

In my mind, I kept telling myself that I was a horrible mother. But that simply wasn't the case. In fact, when the going got tough, my true mom instincts kicked in. In merely two seconds, a fall that could have broken my legs, scarred my girl and caused early delivery of the new addition to our family didn't go the way it could have. Somehow my belly never hit the ground. And somehow my sweet girl was actually held up by merely a centimeter by my thigh, keeping her completely safe and away from the impending danger. Somehow, I just hurt my physical body, and both of my sweet babies were scratch-free.

One could look at this incident as an accident. I saw it as a miracle. I still can't figure out how I landed with the bumps and bruises I got and can't articulate how I had any strength to hold my daughter up that mere centimeter. To me, that was through the grace of God and my family's guardian angel. That day, I realized that my ongoing nightly prayers had been answered. God knew I would prefer to take a beating any day if it meant that my kids were safe, healthy and happy.

The "could haves" and "would haves" turned into a meaningless untrue story that I could opt to continue to tell myself — or let go of, realizing God was there every step of the way. Later that day, I watched my daughter laugh and play with her big brother. I listened to the strong heartbeat of my growing baby, tucked safely in my womb, and laughed at all the rolls and kicks I could hear on the monitor. I saw the love in my son's eyes when he told me his sister was okay.

That moment — when my life could have been turned upside-down — I realized more than ever how right-side up it was. Accidents occur every day. We say the wrong thing and hurt others' feelings. We stumble in our thoughts, in our words, in our steps. But I guess it's not so much about the stumble but about the getting up. Not so much about the dismount but about the landing.

Instead of dwelling on the aches, pains and bruising, let's toss up prayers of thanks and praise. Because it's sometimes through our darkest experiences that we learn the most.

CHAPTER 4
You're Never Lost

I got lost that day, which is comical because the area of town I was in was one that I would frequent regularly growing up. But for some reason on that specific day, I couldn't get my bearings around where I was and how to get to where I needed to go.

After a few unnecessary turns, I finally found myself on the right road headed in the right direction to my next stop. I had driven on this road so often that I could probably predict every twist and turn. For me, it had now become a cut through, but decades ago, it took me to a very important end destination: her home.

A humble apartment hidden just a block off the busy road was always filled with such warmth even on the coldest of days, country cookin' you could smell even in the hallway and more love than could ever be described. She made sure of that. You didn't leave her place without a full belly, a full heart and, of course, a piece of candy from her infamous candy bowl.

My grandma was a simple person when it came to what she needed in life. Family, college basketball, her plants and her Bible. She had the greenest thumb around, especially for African Violets, and while she loved your company, if her favorite basketball team was playing on TV while you were over, you betcha it would be the topic of conversation.

While a sports fan I am not, I always loved seeing her get excited when her team scored.

I'm sure you have people and places like this, too. Those where if you close your eyes you can recall nearly every smell, every sight, every feeling, every detail as they each helped shape you as a person. I remember a lot about her humble apartment, a place that housed a woman who is unforgettable.

I remember her couch that was her prized possession. Finally, a comfortable one after her previous piece had been like sitting on concrete. And how a third of her living room was populated with various plants, all of us loving to watch her Christmas and Easter cactuses bloom annually.

I remember her bedroom, and how when I was little she would let me root through her jewelry, sometimes borrowing some. And her kitchen table — small but mighty — always adorned with a full meal consisting of fried chicken and all the fixins'.

My mom always saying to not break anything; my grandma always assuring there was nothing in her home that she was worried about getting broken. I remember her calling me "Sugs" and getting me a simple tin of popcorn for Christmas each year. It was my favorite.

I remember her, so vividly; her red hair and her brown eyes, how tall she was and how I secretly hoped to one day not have to physically look up to her, although I knew I always would in so many other ways. She was a woman of a faith much stronger than most. Her strength was so admirable; her compassion was so contagious; her love was so deep.

That was my "grandma with the candy bowl." I had named her that.

I had been on this road so many times driving to her place to sit on the front porch and talk about life or pick her up and take her to dinner at her favorite buffet early in the afternoon. I even took the city bus on this road to her home in high school when she learned I had a long walk from the previous route to my house. No, no … Grandma could not let that happen. Instead, she insisted that I switch routes, come to her place and she would not only fix me a feast, but we could enjoy each other's company. And her cooking was so good, but the company was always the most satisfying.

That day when I drove down the all-too-familiar road, I was overwhelmed by cherished memories. As I inched closer to the intersection to get to her apartment, I so badly wanted to turn the car and turn back time. I wanted her to be waiting on her front porch. I wanted all to be right again. I wanted her back.

I'm not alone in that want. We all have loved ones we miss dearly and are anxious to get just one more glimpse of or have one more conversation with. I've begged for dreams, and the few where she has appeared are locked in my "don't-ever-forget" place in my mind. I would pay anything to hear her Southern accent once more.

It wasn't a week after she passed that I had a work meeting with an individual I had created a lasting friendship with. Each time we would meet we would laugh together, sharing glimpses into our lives with one another. That day, instead of sharing laughs we shared tears. I tried to smile as I walked in, but I didn't have to say a word for him to see the hurt behind my façade. As I sobbed, I shared how not only did I miss her already, but I was so mad that my kids would never get to know her.

Such a sweet soul my friend was, and that day God gave him the words my soul needed to be comforted by. "She's never gone, Stephanie.

Your grandma, she's a part of you. Your kids will know her because they know you."

Even years later when my lost adventure took me down memory lane, I realized more than ever how right he was. My grandma, the love that she was is a love she will always be — deep within everyone she touched. And while I don't hear her voice anymore, God knows that sometimes I need a reminder that she's never left my side. On those days, I may see a Redbird, a little sign from heaven to let me know that while she's not still here in body, I am never without her.

That day I was meant to get lost. I was meant to approach that intersection and reflect. I was meant to remember … to remember her. While a day doesn't go by that I don't think of her, that day I needed to feel her confidence in me. I needed a little "it's okay Sugs" from that Southern woman who I never caught up to in height.

And just when I felt so lost and alone, I was reminded that she's never left my side. No one has. In fact, our time together is fleeting, and our bodies will tire, but our spirits live on in the lives of others. At our core, we are love.

We are like those beautiful Christmas cactuses that grow from a single seed and bloom in the lives of others in the most unexpected times. Each encounter you have, you leave a piece of you behind, shaping others in ways you will never know. But never for a moment think that you will be forgotten, for the only thing that lasts forever is love, and you are made from its purest form.

In the times you feel most alone, know that your hands are being held tight, arms are wrapped securely around your waist and you're being carried in ways you don't even expect. In your toughest moments, if you take a second to just breathe and look around, you will see those you love most are always with you. They may show up in Redbirds. My grandma would send them; she was a University of Louisville fan! They may be present in the love that's placed in the hearts of your kids or in the memories that are so detailed you can close your eyes and recreate.

You are not alone or lost. Ever. In fact, sometimes when you feel the most lost, you're actually the most found.

CHAPTER 5

Nothing is by Chance

Although sometimes I feel like I'm on an island, I'm sure there are others who very much live in the same chaos I've deemed normal. But this specific day I felt like even my chaotic comrades would think that I was teetering on the brink of losing it. Possibly I was!

Having three kids poses lots of daily struggles and on top of the basics of "who goes where when" my husband and I are constantly outnumbered. Our life is wild enough on good days when everyone eats their dinner, doesn't irritate each other and gets to bed at a decent hour. So, throw in a sick kid, or three, and it was bound to upset the applecart. This day was a perfect example of just that.

I had been to the pediatrician multiple times in a short timespan with each kid independently, so when my youngest was sick yet again, the mere string holding me together started to unravel. The pediatrician allowed us to take the last appointment slot of the day, one I suspect she made just for us knowing that we needed it dearly. I'm sure she had had a long day, too, and was counting the minutes until it was time to turn off the lights, step away from the germs and head home to see her little ones. But she never showed it.

She walked into the patient room, sat down on the rolling chair and scooted close to me and my youngest. Instead of investigating the culprit for his cough, she turned and looked at me. Two sentences were all it took for me to come completely unglued right there.

"Stephanie, are you doing okay? Have you lost some weight?"

Once the tears started, I couldn't hold them back. It was like the muscles in my eyes were paralyzed as she willingly let me gush the challenges that I had been facing.

She didn't just hear my words; she listened to my cry for help.

She didn't shuffle me along; she put down her chart and told me that she would stay for as long as I needed.

There are some people who are so genuine that all you have to do is look them in the eyes to see them for all that they are. This doctor was the epitome of that all wrapped up into one person, and that day, as she looked at me, I saw her caring spirit and her belief that I could get through it.

After I came up for air from what I can only describe as an embarrassing meltdown, she put her hand on my shoulder and went out on a limb to offer me help. She wasn't sure of my faith but knew I was a believer. She told me that she had no idea how close her church was to me, but that she felt at that moment she needed to tell me about a Bible study that was just for women that would be starting in a few weeks and she'd love for me to join her.

No, she didn't think I was crazy, or at least if she did she didn't say those words exactly. But she did see I needed something, and what better way to provide help than spiritual healing. This Catholic girl, who can't recite a Bible verse if her life depended on it, had no clue what to expect at a Bible study, and especially one outside of the Catholic faith. But something in my heart told me I needed this.

I was late getting to the first session and was completely unprepared, to say the least. I walked into a room of women who all looked put together, ready to learn and to share. Me … that string that was holding me together was just as frayed as it had been before and all I could do was pray that no one else in the room noticed.

We did introductions, and when the Bible study book was handed to me, my heart nearly stopped. Some parts of the Bible hold special meaning to me, and one verse specifically has double meaning as it was the inspiration for the song sung at both of my grandparent's funerals. This Bible study, which I knew very little about, was dissecting the Bible verse that meant so much to me: Psalm 23. Together, we were charged with learning to trade panic for peace by understanding each word that God spoke through this verse.

> *"The Lord is my shepherd, I shall not be in want. He makes me lie down in green pastures, he leads me beside quiet waters, he restores my soul. He guides me in paths of righteousness for his name's sake. Even though I walk through the valley of the shadow of death, I will fear no evil, for you are with me, your rod and your staff, they comfort me. You prepare a table before me in the presence of my enemies. You anoint my head with oil, my cup overflows. Surely goodness and love will follow me all the days of my life, and I will dwell in the house of the Lord forever."*
>
> *– Psalm 23*

While I was unprepared for the first session, I made a pact to myself that I would be prepared for the rest. I learned about what a shepherd does and how finicky sheep are. I learned the analogy of Jesus as our shepherd was no coincidence. It didn't take long for me to feel the panic slip away and for peace to make its residence in my heart. You should always follow doctor's orders, and our kid's pediatrician knew just what my soul needed.

This peace had a new emotion attached to it. It was one of nervousness and excitement woven together. Like that feeling when you are going up on a roller coaster; that anticipatory sensation right before you go over the edge; right before you take a leap of faith.

I had been writing for a while, in my limited spare time. I had felt called to put my thoughts on paper, and I had written a few chapters for a book I envisioned for the future. What I had written, I had not shared with many people. It was so personal, and to be honest, I was scared of rejection. But when one of the chapters in our Bible study connected closely with a chapter I had written, I emailed the leaders and asked if I could share it with the group, feeling as though it was time to take that leap and share.

That feeling of anticipation I'd felt the first time I'd set foot in the church I felt yet again on the night that I was to read my chapter to the group. Speaking in front of others was never a worry of mine, but that night my knees were shaky, and my voice wasn't much better.

I shared with the group about my bucket list dream to publish a book and read one raw chapter to them. Then, as quickly as I had walked to the podium, I returned to my seat. I tried to not make eye contact with anyone. It was scary reading my chapter, but even scarier waiting for the reaction. Or worse … no reaction.

The lady sitting next to me had scribbled on a paper, and I thought she was making a note to recall later, but she ripped the note out and pushed it my way. A name. Two words written on a crumpled piece of notebook paper. As we moved to the next section of our study, she whispered that a single person would propel my dream into reality. And it did. That name was the name of a woman who helped give me the courage and guidance to write and publish this book!

Nothing happens by chance. Nothing. My mental breakdown was meant to happen that day at the pediatrician's office with that specific doctor who was willing to stay late to listen to me. I was meant to join that Bible study group for so many reasons, but especially to write my book as that crumpled up piece of paper housed the name of a soon-to-be book mentor.

Our lives are like those "Choose Your Own Adventure" games we all enjoyed as a kid, except every move we make is critical to shaping who we become. It may be safer to choose the path that you know, but a risk may be just what you need. The risks may be uncomfortable. You may get sweaty hands or experience your voice quivering.

Sometimes it's in your weakest moment that you find your true destiny.

Just when I thought I was unraveling, God was actually helping me build a new beautiful tapestry that I was meant to share.

SECTION 2

ORDINARY MIRACLES

They are all around you, these "God moments." Few may resound like a thundering cloud as depicted in the Bible, but most will not. Most occur as little blips in your day seemingly so minuscule that you may miss them altogether if you aren't open to seeing them. But He strategically seats the right people in the right places at the right time, right when you need them. Your only charge is to remain open to being part of these ordinary miracles.

No, Thank You

You Will Never Be Hungry

Walking Angels

Be the Bow

The Redbird

CHAPTER 6

No, Thank You

I've always had a soft spot for helping others, and I've even been known to guilt those I love into joining me in crazy endeavors to accomplish that, including weekend roadblocks to raise money to fund cancer research.

I didn't look forward to the long, hot summer days, but I enjoyed walking up and down the road, meeting people while collecting donations. I loved hearing stories of those grateful for our dedication — because they had a connection to the cause — and I loved meeting others whose silence taught me that sometimes scars are too deep for words.

You see, when you have your foot on the pavement, your hand out and open and a smile on your face, you strip away all of who you think you are. It doesn't matter where you live, what you drive or what you can afford. The people you meet honestly just care about why you are there and what your purpose is.

In some crazy way, when you remove all of what we think defines us, you begin to get a sense of who you really are, especially when miracles happen right in front of you.

With a fundraising goal to meet and multiple weekends booked, I tried to motivate my teammates even as the weatherman forecasted another hot summer day ahead. This one weekend, the mid-day heat was bound to run away even the strongest of heart. A few people bailed before the day even started, but my trusty dependables — my husband and my dad — came out and promised to try the best they could.

That first hour was hard, but the second hour was harder. My dad, even with frequenting the ice cooler for what I'm sure were much-needed breaks, was fading and no motivational speech was going to keep him going. I waited for the moment when he would say it was time for him to pack up, so when I saw him walking my way, I knew what was about to happen. But something was different. The 6-foot-plus, rugged motorcycle guy had a softness to him, and I saw a rare tear in his eye.

I was right; he had decided he couldn't do any more. He was exhausted and "too old for this" in his words. He had spent the past several traffic light changes thinking through how he was going to tell me he couldn't make it through another two hours of this laborious work but decided to do one last round of collection before he called it a day.

He went down the lanes, car to car, to see who would be his last donor, when he came up to a van. A woman rolled down her window and asked what the cause was about that he was collecting for. Dad looked up and noticed that the light was about to change, so he had to make it quick. "The cancer society," he told her.

She pulled out some change and Dad thanked her for her contribution with a simple "Thank you" and a smile. Then the lady looked Dad right in the eyes, lifted her hand to her head, pulled back her wig and spoke three simple words that my dad will never forget. "No, thank *you*." With that, she drove off.

This woman has no idea the power of what she said or more importantly what she didn't say. Her act of vulnerability that day changed my dad in ways I never could have imagined. This woman, who was undergoing chemotherapy, gave my dad a purpose. We weren't just there for donations or exercise or personal satisfaction when we reached our goal. No, we were there to offer hope to those who maybe didn't have it. Or were we the ones who were struggling with hope that very day?

After that, Dad went back to his spot and made it two more hours. How could he walk away from his new purpose? He had to make it for her, and every roadblock after he paid tribute to the lady whose name he didn't know.

When he got in his truck to head home, waiting at the light where an hour earlier we had been collecting donations, my dad noticed a bumper sticker on the car in front of him. The sticker read "God helps those who help others."

I am sure each of us has uttered words to a friend or stranger that may be meaningless to us. Simple words such as "thank you" or "God bless." Other days, maybe it's a smile, or holding the door open for someone or pulling off your wig.

Our little words and actions impact others whether we know it or not. They change lives even if our lives may be seemingly unchanged.

What if you could completely alter the life of another through a small act of vulnerability? Would you do it? Maybe instead of saying, "You're welcome" when someone thanks you for a kindness, you turn it around and tell them "No, thank *you*."

CHAPTER 7

You Will Never Be Hungry

I like to think I'm a risk taker. I've whitewater rafted and snow skied more times than I can count and enjoyed the wind in my hair while parasailing. I've had three kids so that in and of itself means a life full of unexpected risks. Yet for years I couldn't find the courage to attempt a full mass outside the confines of my church's "cry room."

The room was cozy, and many times dimmed to help those of us who hadn't had enough caffeine yet to slowly ease into the day with a healthy dose of scripture and babbling toddlers. We may not have always heard every reading or been able to let the homily fully sink in, but we were there.

And we were not alone. I found comfort in the other families in that room, all of whom were experiencing life in similar ways as we were. Over the years, my husband and I had watched others who shared the cry room add more little ones to their families and celebrated the new families who were brave enough to enter the germ-filled room with their newest addition.

We shared clothes and advice — and a few sneezes too — but my favorite was the "puffs."

It was a prerequisite in this room to put aside any notion of mine vs. yours. Let's be honest … nothing is more desirable to a little kid than whatever it is that another little kid is holding or playing with or eating. We would ensure each Sunday that we had something our kids could munch on when a book wasn't going to get them through. The usual snack of choice? A canister of puffs.

If you've had kids in the past decade, you probably know what I'm referencing. Those who don't, well you're missing out. Go buy yourself a tube of these minimally flavored little air puffs, and snack on them when you watch your next movie rental accompanied by silence, something that none of us who know puffs — and I mean *really know* puffs — experience regularly, if at all.

Kids must have special superhero skills that we adults lack — like their ability to hear the slight pop of plastic when the lid is removed. Whatever it is, many a tube of puffs fed the tummies of friends that were made in this little room.

The first time that we had interest from other kids in the room, this momma got nervous that we would run out of the puffs quicker than the final "Amen," and that was bound to set the stage for disaster. But it was a risk we were going to take because no one can turn down those pitiful eyes, yearning for their fix of the puff catnip. Of course, we would share. If my kids were supposed to share, I needed to model that behavior myself.

A funny thing happened; we never ran out. I mean, the tube did empty, but no matter how many kids on a given day were patiently waiting, once the lid was popped the anticipated puff meltdown never happened. Each kid was always full enough. The puffs served their purpose.

It's a miracle to me how that would happen, but I guess miracles aren't so far-fetched when you get the chance to actually listen to the scripture instead of appeasing a tantrumed kiddo. My one little puff tube had fed four or five kids, but Jesus was able to feed 5,000 with five loaves and two fish.

No matter what He had, He gave. No one would be turned away or would leave hungry whether body, mind or soul. All were fed; Jesus made sure of it. And I think He continues to in more ways than we will ever know.

Puffs are by no means fish or bread, but I do think that something magical happened each Sunday in that cry room. While my kids learned the face-value of sharing, they also learned the hidden meaning of it as well, how when we give we get so much more in return. Our bellies were all satisfied, and we got to be among friends as we shared puffs. We were one — one crying hot mess sometimes, nonetheless, we came, we prayed and we loved.

No one is perfect, but the perfect One left endless teachings for us. Some we can read about in the Bible, but others hit home as they are experienced. Jesus promised that when we believe in Him, we will never be hungry. We will always be satisfied. If a tube of puffs can prove that, imagine what a life of belief in Him will do for you.

CHAPTER 8

Walking Angels

I am a firm believer that there is a special place in heaven saved for some people, like those who stand up for injustices or the voiceless and those who help another for no personal gain. It's these individuals who you don't question one bit if their admittance ticket will be accepted.

You know those people live their lives for others. They help those in need without question and love unconditionally. If you've met a handful of these walking angels, consider yourself blessed. But even more special is meeting one who doesn't even know that they are an angel.

You can learn a lot from a child. Their innocence gives their words a pureness of true honesty, whether you like it or not.

They are passionate on both sides of the spectrum — when they love unconditionally and when they despise everything in their sight. As they feel out the world, their self-centeredness is usually on high alert. So, when you find one who puts aside their need for personal gain to live to the extreme of love, you've found a gem. When that person is a 5-year-old, you've hit a gold mine.

My son was full of more energy at that age than I could have dreamed of, and smart was an understatement when describing him. So, when we had an opportunity to get him into a structured academic setting earlier than expected, we jumped at the chance.

Academically, he soared at school, absorbing everything thrown at him while loving every second. But maturity-wise, he had plenty of room to grow. We had a family mantra each morning that consisted of daily reminders to keep our hands to ourselves, to say nice words, to not push friends and to follow directions. Most days it worked, but some days, the pent-up little boy inside couldn't be restrained anymore, and we would get a note home from school. One Friday, I heard first-hand from a classmate.

Each week, parents had the opportunity to read to the class after lunch. I'd promised myself to be involved with my kids at their school, so I was excited when the calendar reminded me it was my day to enjoy a lunch at school and read to his class.

I smiled at lunch, but behind my expression I was overwhelmed as all the kids in his class found some way to be the center of my focus. When the newness of my presence wore off, I was left with one girl standing by my side. I noticed her inching closer and closer, and when she realized that she would have my full attention, she lifted her sleeve and showed me a boo-boo on her arm. I quickly asked if she was okay. She smiled and said she was but told me that the mark was because my son had recently pushed her.

My heart sunk. I wanted to spew out every apology possible and take back her hurt. But she touched my shoulder, and almost as if she could tell how apologetic I was, told me she was fine.

As if I was a kid in the class myself, I lined up with the rest when it was time to head to the classroom for me to read. While the rest of the class weaved in and out and down the stairs, I noticed that the little girl found me again in that line. As we made the last turn from the staircase to the hallway with a direct shot to the classroom, I was startled as I felt something on my hand. In a split second, I had a rush of emotion as the feeling felt familiar. As a mom, I'd had little hands wiggle their way into mine before. This sweet girl looked up at me and smiled.

A new friendship was made, and it was one based on something that I didn't know a 5-year-old had the capacity to fully feel or even to give. She didn't know me other than I was the mom of the kid that had most recently hurt her feelings (and her arm). While she should have probably associated negative thoughts with me, she proved that she was different.

That day she embodied the true essence of forgiveness, something most adults struggle with. She showed that even in the depths of hurt, anyone can overcome it by fully "letting go and letting God."

She didn't dislike my son or me for that matter. In one touch, in one handhold, in one sheepish grin, she forgave without ever speaking the word. Her place in heaven is set, no doubt about it in my opinion. Yours is too; I believe that as well.

But until she gets to slide on rainbows and bounce on clouds, she has a job to do. Here. We all do. While I don't know what she will be when she grows up or if I will even get the chance to watch her do it from the sidelines, I do know one thing. That sweet girl is a walking angel. Each of us has the capacity to follow in the footsteps of that innocent and forgiving little girl.

CHAPTER 9

Be the Bow

The chaotic mix of stress that stems from work, home responsibilities and schlepping kiddos is enough to drive anyone to the brink of insanity. I have been to that brink, but every time before I tumble a moment is strategically placed as if it were a rope God offers for me to grasp as he pulls me to safety. These moments aren't angelic in the sense of burning bushes or bright lights. My moments are much more minuscule, taking place at the tiniest of levels that may be overseen if I weren't looking for them.

We all have our quirks about us, and for some reason, a long stare or uncomfortable silence between me and another person will elicit my uncontrollable eye wink. I don't always know I do it and typically do it before I can catch myself. It's not one of those creepy winks, I promise. Just one that means I see you, I really see you, and that for a brief second, all is good in the world for the simple fact that we just shared a moment.

I don't know when it started, but I'm glad that it did. It became a ritual of sorts, especially when we were in the van together. It didn't matter how intense the noise was at that time, my daughter would sit in the back typically very quiet and always patiently watching. As the van would take on every bump and turn, I would glance at the rearview mirror to look at her. Each time our eyes would meet, she'd be looking at the mirror, too. She was always looking for our moment.

When we'd connect, I would no longer dwell on the latest worry on my mind. I would just see her and smile. Our moments would consist of a simple gesture, a simple "wink blink." My quirky tick became a treasured experience with her. While she hadn't perfected the one-eye wink, her purposeful returned eye blink confirmed that even though at that young age her words may have still been difficult to understand, no words were necessary to know that we saw each other for who we were, at that moment, and nothing else mattered but our love.

Love has always been evident in many ways in our home. From wink blinks to slobbery kisses, I take any act of love I can get with my children, knowing our days were numbered until doing so would be embarrassing.

My oldest always had fun getting creative, so one night after reading, I tweaked our nighttime ritual to add some giggles to our bedtime routine. When our eyelashes touched, we shared an angel kiss and we touched ears, imagining that's how elephants kissed as well. If we've had a bad day, all we need to do is put our fingers out for a finger kiss. Each kiss was a part of our secret language, and each proved that God knew just the right moment when we needed a little love from above through someone here and now.

You know how you find it nearly impossible to not tap your foot to the sound of a catchy tune or hum the chorus of your favorite ditty? Well, my youngest couldn't hold back at all. When he would hear sounds that resembled music, a feeling deep within him would stir, and from the tip of his head to his sweet little toes he'd start moving, swaying and bouncing to the rhythm with a smile that could turn anyone's upside-down-day right-side up.

He would dance to anything with a repetitive noise. His favorite was a bouncing ball. He would bring a brightly colored ball for me to bounce. As I started, he would bounce with the beat. He would smile, and by the end of my dribbles, I'd be smiling, too. Our moment together always showed me how simple it is to smile when you feel the calling deep within.

We don't always see Him. Well, at least not the old man in a white beard or His Son in ways that we would expect. But He sees us.

Many times, His eyes come adorned with long, thick, black lashes surrounding deep eyes that glisten even when the sun has set for the day. He's staring at us in the mirror, waiting for us to connect and "wink blink" back.

Many times, His kisses come in a variety of sorts — from angel kisses to toe tickles. He's waiting to slap a big juicy kiss on our cheeks, and while we may want one of those, sometimes it's more of the Mom-not-in-front-of-my-friends kind of ones that are unexpected.

Many times, He is ready to dance even when there is no music. Deep in our soul, He plants the tune, but it's our choice if we listen for it. He doesn't care how silly it makes us look or whether we have a lick of rhythm. He wants to hand us a ball to dribble so we can dance together.

He's all around us. He's in every moment, but sometimes He shares special ones with us to let us know that He sees us. He loves us. For who we are today; for teetering on the brink of doubt. For forgetting how to trust. He loves us the same. It's in these moments with those around us that He takes away the white flag we are waving and lets us know He's got it covered. One-hundred percent.

As much as these moments with my kids have been critical to my life, the same is true for them. As much as I feel loved, connected and joyous … they, too, feel it. That's what's so amazing about these moments — they are free flowing and touch us all equally.

Cherish these moments you're given. Winks, kisses, dances … These are gifts from Him that don't come in a packaged box.

But they do have a beautiful bow, the vessel they are shipped through. You can be that vessel. Be the bow and share your present with others. A wink, a touch or a smile can make all the difference.

CHAPTER 10
The Redbird

Being from Kentucky, no matter how hard you try to dodge it, college basketball is baked deep in your soul. You learn young that the colors red and blue, synonymous with competing sports teams, go together in the same way as oil and water … they don't mix.

I was one of those "in-betweens" who couldn't care less. My mom and my grandma always enjoyed their evenings glued to the television cheering on the University of Louisville Cardinals. But no amount of peer pressure instilled in me a passion for the team, which was a good thing because I happened to marry a passionate University of Kentucky fan. So, while red is in my genes, blue is what lives in our house.

My grandma, one of the University of Louisville's biggest fans I'm sure, was sick for a year. When our family heard the word "cancer," great devastation hit with the thought of it taking her from us. But she fought hard, probably harder than she ever expected to, as she underwent surgery and attempted chemo. While appearance-wise it may have impacted her look — she lost the beautiful red hair that was her staple — I hope she knew that it never defined who she was. She was more than anything a curler could control. She was love in its purest form.

I remember a conversation my mom, my grandma and I had together one evening. My mom shared that she had noticed a bird hovering in the sky while she was driving. After she saw one, she noticed another. She felt peace as something in her heart told her that her dad and her grandma were there with her, flying by her side, promising never to leave.

Considering the birds that my grandpa had sent to my mom, I asked my grandma what kind of bird she would send us. A cardinal, of course.

It wasn't a day or so after she passed that she lived up to her promise. It was as if every Redbird had migrated to the city because everywhere I would look they would be looking back. On a country road, they would be strategically placed on a limb to catch my eyesight. On the interstate, where a tree wasn't in view, one would fly across the road. I'd find bumper stickers purposefully placed for me to get a glimpse and be warmed by the peace of knowing right then and there, she was within reach.

No matter where I was, a cardinal would appear at the precise moment I needed it. When I found out I was pregnant, they came in droves. And when the pregnancy took a turn, they didn't stop. The day I found out I was losing one of my children to a miscarriage, a Redbird flew to sit on the shallow window sill of my kitchen. She turned and looked directly at me for several moments. Time stopped as I knew it was her. She had sent me a message, and that day I heard it loud and clear.

When it was the day to deliver my oldest child, I was terrified of feeling joy because the previous miscarriage left me unconvinced that this joy wouldn't be ripped away too. Even the epidural couldn't take away my ache deep within. It wasn't until the nurse walked in that I felt an immense peace. Out of all the nurses that worked in that department at that hospital, that day that nurse working that shift had decided to wear that pair of scrubs. The pattern I will never forget, a series of Redbirds playing in the snow adorned her.

You would think seeing so many cardinals over the years I would always know I'm not alone.

But probably like you, if it doesn't slap me in the face daily I tend to forget the most basic thing God has always promised. A promise that He has never and will never leave us.

Years after that glorious day my grandma was with me at the delivery of a healthy baby boy, I sat around a noisy dinner table blessed with two more children and a lot more stress. Having multiple kids, I'd learned how to tune out noise to get by. While that was helpful during dinner time, it's not so helpful when you are looking for God to direct you.

I'd had a challenging day, having my energy zapped from things out of my control and my passion questionable as I was finding it hard to see God's plan. I knew in my heart where He wanted me to go, but I couldn't figure out the most direct path to get there. So, I took a moment to breathe and prayed the only prayer I could find the words to say. "*Help me.*"

It was like it was on repeat. "Help me. Help me, Lord, to see You. Help me to feel You. Help me to know I'm not alone. Help me to know You are by my side. Help me to find the path You want me to go down. Help me be the me You know me to be. Lord, help me."

Then I picked myself up and finished my day as best as I could, but it didn't get easier. A stomach bug found me trying to just make it until it was time to give in and take a rest. The kids were fed, and giggles echoed through the house as usual. They filled my heart with the strength

I needed to get through what the rest of the day had drained from me. Then right before bed, as I sifted through my oldest son's classwork that had been sent home, I spotted it.

I didn't always get the chance to see them in nature, so God again had to get a tad creative to send me a message. And there is no doubt He did that night. At the bottom of the pile was an abstract birch tree my son had painted with a red piece of construction paper taped to one of the branches. It had been folded to fit into his backpack, but it only took a moment after I opened the page to let the miracle sink it.

A Redbird. Just when I needed it most, had found its way into my home. I didn't even know that my son knew of such birds, and I know he hadn't a clue of their meaning to me yet. Every detail of the precisely cut-out cardinal was meant as a sign from God that all would be well. I prayed for help that day, and He gave it to me, loud enough where there was no way to not accept it.

Some may call it coincidences — my Redbird sightings — but I believe they are so much more. Maybe in some houses in the South, red and blue do clash, but in our house where we bleed blue, we will always cherish our Redbirds.

SECTION 3

PERFECT IMPERFECTION

Nothing is ever perfect, and yet it all always is. Your day may not go as you have precisely planned or you may be able to find flaws in others and in yourself, but just because to you, things aren't perfection, know that to God everything is. He made you. He made today. Everything He touches is designed just the way He intended it to be.

Do Your Best

You Get to Choose

Making Memories

I See You

Your Voice

CHAPTER 11

Do Your Best

If I could schedule a coffee (or chai tea, in my case) with my younger self, I'd have a lot to tell her. Like how those oversized sweatshirts never did any favors for her figure or the belief that being tan was better than being pale was really a marketing ploy and would one day cause wrinkles. She definitely would need to know that she will go through heartache, and that ache will hurt in ways she can't imagine. Some of it will linger and never truly disappear, but she will make it through.

I wish I could have helped prep her for experiences she would endure, both the painful and joyous ones. What I would give to knock her up-side the head and help her focus on what would propel her forward, who was worth her time and what path she needed to take to get to her end destination more quickly.

But it doesn't work that way. There is no time machine or teleportation mechanism to reverse what's been done. And I'm sure that's totally by design. I mean, look at things we can reverse, like our cars. We can drive backward, but in doing so, think about how challenging it is to drive a straight line, to not twist and turn.

I have always been a perfectionist. While it sounds good on paper, at times it can be debilitating, especially in school. The moment I stepped foot into a classroom, I couldn't absorb enough of what the teachers gave for my liking. I was a learning junkie, but one that had to be perfect at it.

My need to excel started young, and no matter how much I tried, it became who I was, and dictated my life so much that most weekends of my childhood you could find me with my face in books as I tried to relearn everything I needed for an upcoming test. Once I started to get the positive reinforcement of straight A's, I couldn't allow myself to stop. The competition that ran in my veins became one with myself.

My parents were proud at first, until they noticed how what had begun as a passion for learning had evolved into a fear of failure. With that fear came an unhealthy dose of sleep deprivation as I constantly attempted to cram for tests in lieu of getting needed rest. It worked, I guess. I completed school with all A's and added salutatorian and valedictorian to my list of accolades. I graduated college with my head held high, but while those two decades of my life I'd done what I set out to achieve, it didn't take long to realize at what expense.

A few days into my first job I realized that no one cared about what I had made my lifelong priority. Those days that I had gotten up early even amidst sickness and gone to school to ace that test. Those nights that I opted to study versus hang out with my friends. None of it mattered now. Yes, you could say my work ethic and dedication helped me land a job. But would one "B" on a test have changed my life? Come on young Stephanie … didn't you know that?!

It didn't take long for me to see perfectionism stirring in my kids. That inherited trait had been passed down whether I wanted it to or not. Even without my saying a word, they felt like doing okay wasn't good enough. It had to be great. *But it doesn't have to*, I now know, and while I can't have a candid conversation with my younger self, I can lay the foundation for who I need to be for my kids in the years to come. That starts today, with being honest with myself. Maybe my honesty will help you be honest with yourself as well. So here it goes:

Always remember that no one is perfect, no matter how hard anyone tries, at least not in the way we typically think. Even when you thought you were, you weren't. The glorious thing about that is, it's okay. It's okay to not know everything, to make mistakes, to fail. Because, as we all have learned the hard way, it's in our failed attempts that we grow the most. Some of your biggest mistakes have taught you more than when you glided by.

As a parent, make sure that your kids have opportunities to fail, and when they do, sometimes let them try to stand up on their own. Be there, of course, but the best thing you can do for them is teach them how to fly.

Secondly, don't be so hard on yourself. Life is too short to worry about what you could have done. Focus on what you can do now. Take every experience as a learning one and concentrate your energy on what you can control. Speaking of which, you don't have to do as much as you think you do. Actually, a lot of things in life are out of your hands, and that's by design. Have faith and know that you are where you are because that's where you are supposed to be. Your kids are bound to end up on a path that you may not have paved or ever ventured on, but that doesn't mean it's not the right one for them. Love them nonetheless.

Finally, be okay with okay. Stop competing with yourself. Learn when excellence is necessary and when "good" is enough.

Don't get wrapped up in the wrong concerns but get wrapped up in what's worth the investment. Pat yourself on the back when you do something worthy of praise but realize that it's not about simply celebrating the outcome. It's also about the work ethic you put in, the passion you exuded and the excitement around the possibilities ahead. Stop trying to exceed for name's sake, and instead do your best. Your kids will need you to be this example for them.

No, we can't go backward. No matter how much of a pro you are in backing into a parking space, your reverse skills beyond that are null and void. Drive forward and do so with purpose and intent. Be the person you want others to emulate. Celebrate what matters, so those you love most know what is worth your energy. Show your kids what it looks like to fail, so they know how to grow from it. Praise them for doing their best, even if it means not reaching the societal standards or even their own expectations. Love them anyway. For one day, they, too, will look back and realize that while Father Time isn't on their side, you always will be.

CHAPTER 12

You Get to Choose

The ice skating rink was my happy place for years. When most "tweens" would go to the movies or to the mall on weekend nights, I could be found on the ice. Nothing could compare with a healthy dose of gossip, soft pretzels and Olympic-style spin attempts. When I set foot on the freshly resurfaced ice, I felt like I could tackle anything. My life was complete.

This one weekend was like every other, and that Friday night I needed my ice-fix. The packed rink left me frustrated because I couldn't skate freely at my own pace, and had to flow with the crowd. My friends and I still found speed by weaving in and out of the beginners. That night, as we were feeling adventurous, my friend made a quick decision to jump in front of me as we approached a tight spot.

I remember not being able to stop. I remember falling flat and sliding for what felt like the length of the rink. I remember the embarrassment. My friends were going so fast that the crowd swallowed me up. Panic set in when I looked on the rink, and instead of seeing opaque ice, it was tinged red. The pain came after I attempted to stand and couldn't. It wasn't until my jeans were cut off my leg that I pieced the story together. As my friend prepped for speed, I stumbled onto her blade, and for a split moment, the blade and I united by way of my knee.

Ten stitches and a leg brace not only kept me from feeling the rush on the ice, but also the ease of walking. I struggled with little things I had taken for granted merely days before, like taking a shower or navigating the stairs between classes in high school. While my inability was temporary, the memory is long-lasting.

Years later, when I heard my son scream after jumping into a tent made of blankets, I was in denial that he, too, may have experienced what temporary inability would be like. After an hour of him not moving much and coddling his arm, an ER visit was critical, and after multiple x-rays, it was confirmed that it was broken.

At first, he liked the attention, probably like I did when I was whisked away like a fallen princess off the ice. Concern showed up in extra hugs, one-on-one attention and friendly smiles. Who wouldn't welcome that? But once reality set in, the "coolness" of a cast or a brace wasn't really so cool after all.

My son loved intricate toys at his young age, and to play with them to their fullest capacity required two hands. He loved to draw, but he needed both hands — one to draw and one to hold the page. He loved playing make-believe with his sister, and yet I overheard him tell her that he couldn't play "clean up" because he only had one hand and needed two to hold the broom. Even going to the restroom required two functioning hands.

For a kid, his world was rocked. His little life which was already complicated as he was still learning, was impacted now that he had an arm that was more of a hindrance than a help. At least to me, it was. But he didn't stop a beat. You would think that he would have gotten frustrated by his inability to open a banana or get in and out of his bunk bed. You would think he would have complained about his "large Band-Aid," but he didn't. He actually didn't complain at all, and while he did ask for help, most times I had to prompt it. Instead, he figured out his new life, and found it just as fulfilling as before.

He definitely knew that one of his arms wasn't in use, but he wasn't stopped by this inability. Instead, he was thrilled that his other arm worked! He still played and jumped and did things that stressed me out, but he was more cautious and even told me that he needed to watch what he did because if he broke his other arm, he wouldn't have any arms to use! I found myself secretively watching him navigate his world, and one day, observed him trying to eat his afternoon snack in the car. Somehow, he'd figured out how to hold a bowl and eat his snack all while not dropping it on the floor and maneuvering in ways I wouldn't have known to do myself. His seeming inability was anything but.

The day I got the stitches out of my knee in high school was a day I had counted down to. I broke free of the leg brace and, while timid to bend my knee again; I was thrilled I could semi-normally walk.

You don't realize what you have until you lose it. I didn't realize how important my legs were until I couldn't use them like I was used to. I had taken them for granted, much like we all do for many things in life — like the ability to talk or eat or even breathe.

Not everyone has those abilities. And when my son got his cast off, he too was thrilled to be able to have his arm back. Grateful for healing, of course. But my son's experience taught me that just because I saw something as an inability didn't mean he did. His gratefulness was planted the moment the break occurred. He was thrilled he had another arm that worked! It didn't stop him from trying to build tents, color pictures or help others as he always had. His life continued, and he was grateful he got to experience it.

We all tend to let things hold us back in life. We aren't Van Gogh, so we don't even try to paint. I'm no Stephen King, so maybe I should stop writing. You're scared of screwing up parenting, so you don't even talk about having a family. We are so stifled by what we see as our inabilities that we don't even attempt to try. We focus on our weaknesses so much that we lose sight of our strengths.

My challenge to you is this. If you have your hands, paint! If your hands can't do it, use your toes! Whatever you make will be a work of art. If you have a thought, put it down on paper. Capture it. Who cares about typos or correct grammar? You may touch one person by your story, and if you do, then it's worth it. And when you have kids, they don't come with a handbook that's for sure. You will screw up, but you'll learn, and your life will be fulfilled in ways no one can describe.

Be grateful for what you do have and focus on those things that you actually have the opportunity to impact. You can't control everything — I couldn't pad my son from his fall. But I can control my perspective on the situation. While I hated that he had a broken arm, I was thankful he didn't break both! My leg may not have been functional for a time, but the time was brief, and I hadn't broken my knee cap, which I was a mere inch from doing.

You may not get to choose what life deals you, but you get to choose how you deal with life.

That doesn't mean you have to live in a glass half full or half empty. No, sometimes reality downright stinks, so own that. Accept what has happened, and then choose to not let it stop you. We are here for a brief moment — and if we can see our abilities through our inabilities, then maybe … just maybe … we can be grateful for what we do have, for what we can do and for who we get to experience it all with.

CHAPTER 13

Making Memories

There was a time in my life, before I had kids when crossing large bodies of water and immersing myself in different cultures in new continents was something I experienced in person, and not through watching a documentary. In fact, I've visited quite a few unique and memorable places. France. Spain. Mexico. The Bahamas. Canada. Jamaica. And my favorite, Australia.

Even though my travel experiences are quite different post-kids, vacations are times we get excited about. You can spend time with loved ones while putting your normal routines on hold and experience life in ways like never before. You can forget about daily worries and live in bliss. And while we know that feeling isn't permanent, it's worth every second.

You're making memories that will last a lifetime; ones that leave your heart warm and a smile on your face that can't be wiped off. But memories are finicky little things, and if you think back to some of the most memorable experiences you've ever had, it's actually not those that you would have thought your brain would have saved space for. In fact, when things in life go as planned, you may not recall each detail about the experience vividly, but you'll probably remember the feeling you had at the time. However, when your experience has a kink in the system, that memory can't seem to be wiped off the slate.

I was in high school when I first boarded a plane, leaving my family so I could spend a week with people I somewhat knew in places I had only seen in my foreign language textbooks. I am sure the trip to France and Spain was educational, however, what I remember most are a few experiences I wish I'd never endured. I remember calling my parents halfway through the trip in tears as I explained to them that while everyone else was taking in the scenery and practicing their language skills, I had had nearly every bodily fluid make its way on me.

It started the moment I set foot on the long flight. It wasn't until then that I realized the kid in the seat in front of me hadn't gotten up for the duration of the flight. You see, his decision to not visit the restroom meant that he left me with my backpack, which had been nestled under his seat, sporting an overwhelming urine smell and a lingering stain; my trip didn't feature any washing machines. While the rest of my classmates enjoyed the architecture of Paris, I will forever remember Notre Dame, because it was the place one of the 10,000 pigeons shared their left-over lunch with me by way of a bowel movement all over my clothes. No, those two experiences didn't put me over the edge. But getting puked on by another classmate on the bus ride to Spain did. I was out of clean jeans and sanity. I may not remember the taste of the food or the brush-strokes of the famous artwork in the Louvre, but I'll always remember my multiple misfortunes.

Upon college graduation, my dad and I took a trip around the world, literally, to check Australia off our bucket list. The trip of a lifetime — and one I will definitely never forget! Especially the fact that I nearly lost him in the land Down Under during a time when cell phones were nonexistent; or, the scary moments I had trying to pray in a beautiful Sydney church while a crazed local stood on the alter staring at all in attendance like he would pull out a grenade at any time. Obviously, he was a regular because everyone else continued with the expected knee-stand-sit Catholic pattern, oblivious to this threat. Yes, I will remember the kangaroos and the outback, but I will never forget the hiccups.

Every trip has them, and they aren't ones that holding your breath or a "boo" will fix. In the moment when you're living them, you may be mortified or willing to do anything to adapt the situation. But later, you realize that each leave a lasting impression, and hopefully, most leave you smiling.

I guess a vacation is an analogy for life, right? You plan. You experience. You learn and grow. Sometimes there are tears or laughs, and sometimes there are both at the same time. But if there is one thing that can be guaranteed on both accounts; perfect isn't feasible. No matter how much money we spend, something will go wrong.

Even if perfect was something we could attain, is it really something we would want?

I'll take imperfect any day if that means I got to make memories with my dad, just him and me, as we experienced a world of "no worries" in Australia. And let a bird leave its leftovers in my hair if it means I get to experience learning up close and personal. I'll accidentally eat squid again on my trip to Cancun if it means I get to spend some quality time with my closest friends. And even though the shower sounded like a great place to sleep to drown out my grandma's snoring when I visited Canada with my family, I'll happily listen to her evening noises every day, because in retrospect, I'm grateful that I got to spend time with her — and that she loved me enough to allow me to be a part of her experience, too.

**Making memories isn't about the perfect.
It's about what you do with the *imperfect.***

It's not really about making lemonade out of lemons, but how messy you get, how much sugar you add and how many laughs you bring as you do it. Toss away any expectations you have for life because the only thing you should expect is to expect the unexpected. I tend to think it's during those times that we realize most who is really in control. And I can tell you for sure; it's not us.

Stop stressing about what you want to happen and be grateful that something is happening. Don't sweat over a stain on your backpack, even if it means you reek for a week. Laugh more, even if that means laughing at yourself. Experience more, even if it means taking a chance that something won't go as planned. That's what memories are all about. Take a leap of faith and know that even if something as catastrophic as a hurricane rains on your parade, literally, I can promise you this — you will have a plethora of memories you are bound to never forget.

CHAPTER 14
I See You

As I entered my life post-college graduation, I had an unrealistic expectation of what the "real world" would offer me. I envisioned that my degree would not only open doors that I hadn't even considered, but it would also provide a paycheck that was heavier than the one I had been getting. So, when I accepted my first job, I quickly learned to focus on the opportunities it would give me in the future versus what I would get in the now.

The future looked bright; the present looked bare. By that, I mean bare bones as I accepted a job paying me barely enough to get by. I knew it would be a stepping stone for my career, but at the moment I had to live thriftier than I was already accustomed to living. As a new homeowner, I knew that would be a challenge, so I was more than appreciative inheriting most of my home necessities as hand-me-downs from my dad.

From silverware and towels to a washer and dryer, I took anything he was willing to give. While I used everything he provided to me, the large and outdated TV console outweighed all. The picture was tiny, but I never complained because I knew I couldn't afford a fancy new flat screen which was the newest craze. Thank heavens, though, that I'd saved the little I had because one day I came home to the reality it was time to upgrade.

A combination of an ear-piercing noise vibrating from the console and the hair prickled on my cat proved it was time to brave an electronics store and buy a new one. I researched, and after seeking all options, was elated when I found an amazing online deal. The sale seemed unmatchable but being more comfortable buying something at that price point in a store, to the store we went.

A friendly young man helped me find the TV that would fit perfectly in my house, on top of the dead console because I couldn't afford a stand. But when we started talking price, I couldn't get him to negotiate a discount that would match the online deal. I made it clear my frustration with their lack of price-matching and stormed out, determined to go home and order online. However, when I did, I realized that I had misread the deal and the one the sale associate was going to give me was actually next to perfect.

Instead of being grateful for what had been offered to me, I was rude by its fullest definition.

Being that I had no other option, I realized I had to put my tail between my legs and go back up to the store to take his deal, but I was too chicken to do it. I decided I was going to make my better half go in and apologize for me. He had a way with people, and I hoped that he could get the sales representative back to good graces before I came in to pay. I was so embarrassed that I decided to drop him off while I ran to get something to eat across the street and requested a phone call when he got the deal secured.

I found a fast-food joint, and even though I was sick to my stomach, I decided carbs would make me feel better. I walked up to the door of the restaurant, the recent experience replaying in my mind. Being in no rush to get back to the electronics store, I held open the door to the restaurant for a man and his young child who were behind me, so they could enter first. I smiled — which was hard to do that day — and they smiled back. We walked in, and as we were both looking at the menu, I gestured for them to order ahead of me. Not a big deal for me, but apparently a big deal for him.

After he placed his order, he turned around and looked me straight in the eyes which was the beginning of a short but impactful conversation. "You are a Christian, aren't you?" he said. "I can tell." I paused for a second, not because I questioned my answer but because I questioned the timing. I told him yes and thanked him for his words as that was about all I could sputter out. "God bless" was the end of our interaction. If that wasn't God working in my life, I don't think I could recognize Him if He smacked me in the face.

Here I had been as un-Christian as possible in how I had treated another person, but by merely opening a door, the other customer could identify where my heart typically lies. I wasn't even being purposeful in my actions; in fact, him going in front of me was delaying what I knew I needed to say to the one person I had been downright awful to. But even during one of my lowest points, a stranger looked and saw me for who I was, and he gave me the motivation to do what needed to be done.

I ate my food then, with a pep to my step, made my way back to the store. As I expected, my now husband and the sales associate were laughing when I arrived. I apologized, and he was a good sport about it all, still giving me a good price for a new TV. I left the store thrilled about my new purchase while realizing that I had gotten much more than I'd bargained for.

That day I had made a mistake, and I'm not talking about the fact that I didn't take the original deal.

I had chosen to let the wrong things lead me. I found fuel in frustration instead of love.

But even when I was letting that take over, God took the reins and directed me back on the path to Him. Those few sentences from a man I didn't know reminded me that no matter what you've done or the path you've gone down, anything can be fixed through the grace of God. Anything.

CHAPTER 15

Broken Beautiful

There was a point in my life when the fear of talking to anyone would be nearly crippling. It didn't matter if I was supposed to talk to one person or to a crowd, I would break out in red splotches and clam up. "Shy" was an accurate descriptor of me when I was young, as I would hide behind my parent's legs when approached by anyone. If I did decide to talk, I would squeeze out a squeak as if I could still hide the real me behind a nearly inaudible noise.

My parents knew that deep down within me lived a girl with a voice that needed to be let out and heard, and to help me find the confidence I needed, they signed me up for modeling. Now, there was definitely no hope that this extracurricular would turn into something monetizable as this short, freckled pipsqueak wasn't destined for the runway, but it was a means to an end; meant to push me to live outside my comfort zone. And that it did.

While I despised getting up in front of class or having to place my own order at a restaurant, my squeaky voice subsided and little-by-little I was up for taking a few more risks such as going door-to-door selling candy bars as a school fundraiser.

Rather than doing homework, a friend and I braved the neighborhood on our selling venture. With our box of chocolates nearly empty, I was startled when I heard his voice as we turned to head home. While his presence is definitely never questionable, it took me a second to register my dad as he pulled up in a new ride. A 1998 Ford Mustang.

"Is this the right color?" he had asked. While I still had several years before I would be driving, I had already talked about wanting a blue car, and what I'd find out soon enough was that the joy ride Dad was taking was actually the car that one day would be mine.

Riding in a convertible was fun, but I couldn't wait to be the one behind the wheel. So, when I got my driver's permit, I was willing to try everything to ensure I would be well equipped to pass my test. My parents found a credible driver's education company and signed me up in hopes it would boost my confidence and prepare me for what was to come.

The instructor was to pick me up after school for several sessions and between the drive from school to home he was expected to teach me the skills I needed to be considered a good, safe driver. When the school bell rang, I flew out of the building, elated to see that car, all branded with "Student Driver" so other cars on the road would stay far away from this newbie.

Even though it's been years since that day, I can still recall what it felt like to sit in the driver's seat. Short has its downfalls and driving in a car made for average people was one of them. So, I had to sit on the edge of the seat after it was pushed as far forward as possible just to reach the pedals. I drove off, slowly, as the instructor discussed our game plan.

I remember so many details of that day, but I barely remember him — what he looked like or what his voice sounded like.

To this day, I have pushed that deep within as if to shield myself from the pain of remembering. No, I don't remember him, but I will always remember what he did.

Things started off fine until he made comments less about my driving and more about me. It started by him directing me to the closest park near school, which seemed innocent enough because it had lots of windy roads that gave me great opportunity to practice. However, the instructor had planned it perfectly as several cross-country runners were out with their schools practicing. I didn't think anything of it at first until we came up to a pack of girls running and he asked me to slow down. He watched them run like they were his prey, and his eyes were focused on each girl's attributes instead of their skill. He caught me off guard; I, unfortunately, had obliged.

His comments didn't stop. Once he made one, he gained the confidence he needed for them to flood in. With each comment on how the girls looked in their running gear to the silent stares he gave as if he could peer into what each of the young women looked like underneath them, I became more paralyzed. Even though years before I had been empowered to find my voice, when I needed it most, it was lost. I stopped talking but couldn't stop shaking, and my trembles got worse when his comments turned from women outside the car to the only one inside. He commented on my school uniform, on my appearance's impact to those around me and even touched my leg.

There are a lot of "should-haves" I should have done. I should have told him to stop talking. I should have smacked his hand or his face. I should have sped past the runners or pulled off on the side of the road and gotten out of the car and ran myself. But I didn't. I didn't do anything. I was paralyzed in fear. I had no cell phone, no voice, no hope. I was trapped, and he knew it.

As we ventured closer to home, I panicked. I think he could tell because he started to layer threats in with his inappropriate comments, leaving me with the reminder that he knew where I lived, and he would find me if I ever told anyone anything. As we pulled up to my house, he informed me that he would be coming in whether I invited him in or not.

My mom, who normally worked from home, wasn't there that day and he knew I was there all alone. As that truth set in, I found he had already made his way into my house. Now, alone in my home, I paced while trying to determine a way to get myself safe again. But I couldn't.

He walked down the hall, heading to the restroom to change his clothes for the funeral he had told me he needed to visit next, but decided he'd rather change in the middle of the living room, where he was in my line of sight. Panic set in, and more threats were made, but somehow (perhaps it was God's protective hand), once he was suited in funeral attire, he left.

The house was quiet as tears streamed down my face. And even though I had hoped to feel safe, I honestly didn't feel safe at all. I had been violated, my innocence stolen. The voice I had worked so hard to find, suppressed deep within. My body shook as I found the phone to call my mom to tell her I made it home. Our conversation started simply, but she quickly knew something was wrong without me ever having to say it. At first, I opted not to speak details, but then the sobs came, and I released it all — tears, panic and a fear I'd never known before.

Mom rushed home, and I told her everything. She jotted on a piece of paper each detail I was willing to share and thank heavens she did because as I spoke my truths, my subconscious packaged it all in a box that would be kept deep within me for years to come to compartmentalize the trauma.

We filed a police report but I could see it in the police officer's eyes that he didn't trust a word I said. Little energy was put into looking into my allegations. In fact, it was quite the opposite as I, the victim, was told to keep quiet while my instructor was allowed to continue his business as usual.

No amount of beauty that the convertible would exude would make me want to drive again. It sat in the garage, shiny and tempting, but I had no desire to get behind the wheel. My parents knew if they didn't do something, fear would consume me. So, one day another man in another car picked me up to teach me how to drive. He had been told my story — he knew my trauma — and he was determined to help me overcome it. Together, we did.

Years have gone by since, and I've seen the branded car of the company that was led by the man who stole so much from me. I haven't a clue how many others he's traumatized. I pray none. But I fear more than most will admit.

My voice may have been stifled then. The person who I am today is frustrated by the person who I was that day. Before finding myself the victim of sexual harassment, I would have thought that I would have handled things differently. But until you are in it, you truly haven't a clue your reaction.

That day, one man broke me, or at least he attempted to. I let him for a little bit before deciding no one would stop me from talking. I started by talking to my mom, telling her everything. Then, over the years, I've slowly shared pieces of my story with others. To some, I may seem like a strong-willed woman, but deep down, hidden in a place that only sometimes my mind will let me venture to, is a box. That box, when opened, tells the story of a girl who believed that all people were good but saw differently. That girl trusted and in doing so, trusted the wrong person.

I could have decided to never trust again; to live in fear. That's what he wanted, and that's what I refuse to do.

I may have a piece of me broken; a piece I'll never get back. But from that day forward I've decided to gather all of my broken pieces and build me, albeit a broken version, back together. I've decided to bloom into someone beautiful.

I've decided to not hide my voice but to use it. To tell my story, in hopes that someone somewhere will realize that no matter what has happened, you can choose to become empowered from a place where you feel shattered. You can trust again; you can find hope. I've realized that while there may be some rottenness in this world, it's usually the exception. For there is more good placed around us.

If you're broken, know that you don't have to be. Find your pieces and start putting them back together. They may not be as perfectly placed as they were before, but however they are, the new you will be magnificent, too. No matter where you are planted, make time to grow because when you do, the seed within you will flourish to someone beautiful.

SECTION 4

LIVE LIFE CHILDLIKE

We are born with the gift of a giggle that's contagious, a smile that lights up a room, an ability to love unconditionally and a willingness to forgive others without question. We are gifted with innocence, but as life happens, our perspective can shift it. Don't let it. Take the reins of your life and change course if need be. While experiences may shape you, never abandon the gifts God equipped you with early. Keep close the person deep within that is less calloused and more free-spirited. Choose to let that person shine and live your life more childlike.

The Present

We're More Alike

It's All About the Play-Doh

The Essence of Magic

Be the Reason

CHAPTER 16

The Present

I grew up eating dinner at the bar table in our kitchen where a small TV box was perched on a swivel top. While I didn't always get to pick the station, I did always have my eyes glued to its contents. I turned out just fine if you ask me, but I was determined to limit my kids' screen time when I found out I was pregnant with my first. By the time the third came, I had made sure we had enough TVs for everyone in the car to enjoy. This overprotective momma found it a very important part of our daily survival technique, whether I wanted to admit it or not.

Even if I had wanted to test out a night without the TV turned on, I was sure my kids would have complained. So, I was surprised when a dinner gathering one evening didn't resort to a cartoon debate but instead resulted in conversation.

Because I grew up as an only child, I found myself in adulthood overwhelmed with my large family sometimes. That particular night, because the kids weren't in a TV coma, each was trying to out-talk the next. I sat back and watched, hoping none of them would notice what our evening was missing and, to my surprise, they never did.

In the world of the 24-hour news cycle and in the midst of my own social media addiction, I always struggled to focus on one thing at a time. If

I was cooking, I was also responding to emails. If I was driving, I was on the phone playing catch-up.

Most days, I wouldn't give myself the opportunity to pause and soak up life. But I did that evening. I stopped being enamored with the digital world and focused on the tangible world in front of me.

We laughed together as my kids talked about their days in typical kid-like fashion, and just when the conversation lulled, and I expected the kids to beg for the TV, my oldest took our conversation deeper. "Momma, I wish you and Daddy were both good drawers," he told me. I found this comical as I had never wished for that particular accolade. I hadn't realized how much it meant to him until he begged me to draw him a character of his choosing each night. So, while I giggled under my breath, I replied, "Well Daddy may not like to draw, but he's great at lots of things, isn't he?"

That question started a game that all family members took an interest in. My son looked at his daddy and asked, "Who is the best at putting pictures I color on the door really high?," to which, my husband raised his hand. I did, too, but it was obvious that I wasn't worthy of that praise because the following question was, "Who is the best at putting pictures on the door medium?" I raised my hand at that one while laughing, knowing that was his attempt at a height joke.

The game continued. Who was the best at coloring and dancing? Who was the best at eating dinner and playing with their little brother? As we went around that tightly packed table, I listened closely to each of the kids as they tossed out what they thought was pretty amazing about each person, so that everyone had a chance to raise their hand and get praise. Though the honors may have been silly, the intention was in purest form. Through the mouths of kids, you only get the truth, 100 percent, like it or not.

Even after their bellies were full and we migrated to the living room, the kids never noticed the television remained in hibernation. It wasn't until after we played puppets and puzzles, even until after baths had commenced, that they noticed it was time to watch their favorite show before bedtime. We cuddled together on the couch while viewing the choice cartoon of the week, a Mickey Mouse episode that had been made in the late 60s. No one cared about the poor animation. We just tapped our feet and hummed the tune to the iconic ditty. Together.

I typically have my phone connected to my hip, but that night I didn't have it within grasp. I didn't even want it. Instead, I wanted the kids to scoot even closer on the couch as I cherished the hand that was holding mine and the head that was resting on my lap. I wanted to soak up the present.

The Christmas season was upon us then, so within reach we had a slew of presents already wrapped and waiting –each with a name of a deserving kid anxiously waiting to open and explore their contents. But that night, I realized that we could have had oodles more under the tree, and I wouldn't get the present that I would want most.

That evening where I was free of outside stimuli, I realized that the best present I could get doesn't come wrapped in a box and adorned with bows. It comes from the time spent with those who matter most. It comes in belly laughs and sweet giggles. It comes in drawing cartoon characters begged for and it comes in couch cuddles.

The best present isn't one you buy; it's one you freely give and the one you deeply feel.

No matter the season, give the best gift you could possibly give another. I promise it will fill you up as much as it does others. It won't break or go out of style, and re-gifting is not just okay but encouraged. If you get this present, consider yourself among the lucky because nothing can beat the best present … which is merely *being* present.

CHAPTER 17

We're More Alike

Merely weeks before our first family trip to Disney World, my son got a new "best friend" ... a clunky glow-in-the-dark and soon-to-be smelly plaster cast shielding his broken arm from more disaster. Wishful thinking kept me hoping he would get it off in time for our trip, but sometimes we all need a healthy dose of realism. There was no avoiding the inevitable. The magical trip we had been anxiously counting down to would have an unwelcomed guest.

My son was a trooper, though, determined to not let it impact his ability to enjoy the vacation. In fact, with the cast, he felt invincible like one of the superheroes he admired. To him, the world was still his oyster. I, on the other hand, was a nervous wreck, typical of any mother/son dichotomy. Besides the huffing and puffing when he would get his arm stuck in an awkward position, he seemed to forget the hard plaster encasing his limb. To be honest, I forgot many times too. (That is, until others pointed it out.)

There were two pools at our Florida home-away-from-home. The smaller one seemed like the perfect safe haven for my littles. But after venturing to the big pool equipped with a pirate ship, I couldn't hold my oldest back from exploring it. The doctor promised his cast was waterproof, but I brought a cast cover just in case. Because he planned to play on the pirate ship for hours, I pulled out the skin-tight sleeve, firmly tugged it over the cast and pumped every ounce of air out to seal it.

Quickly, he jumped in and got down to business — making friends. The pool was important, but his goal was to meet other kids, making as many friends as he could. The only time he would break away from playing was when the vacuum seal would break on the cast cover. As air leaked in, he would seek me to come to his rescue.

After a trip down a slide, the seal broke and together we waded through the pool to our bag of supplies. As I attached the pump to his cast cover, I had the feeling I was being watched. Like passing a car wreck, I now realize they couldn't help but to look. Two moms lounging on patio chairs were whispering and taking turns making quick glances at my son and his arm.

I saw their pity and their concern. If the tables were turned, I would wonder the scope of this little guy's injury that was currently masked out of sight. Under the cast was a world of unknown for them, and I could tell they feared the worst. No words were needed as their eyes said it all. They couldn't see past it. They were so engulfed in the "what ifs" and the "oh no's" that they couldn't see what was really happening in front of them. They didn't notice his giddy legs, waiting to make their way back into the water, or his smile that was so wide nearly every tooth was showing. His arm didn't stop him from enjoying all that the pirate ship had to offer. He didn't notice the cast, and neither did any kid he met that day. But their moms did.

The weekend we arrived home from our trip we overslept. It was great for the body, but not good for the soul as we missed our typical and much-needed church time. We opted to visit a neighboring parish later that morning and found our way to our normal spot, the cry room.

We came equipped with the norm: a diaper bag, a stash of snacks and coloring books galore. The kids each picked their treat of choice and cracked open the bag of well-used crayons. Another boy in the room approached my oldest once he'd selected his coloring page, determined to beautify the page as well. I went stiff, unsure as to how my very particular son would react. He must have remembered the definition of sharing because he embodied it at that moment.

The two boys colored for quite some time before they spoke to one another, but it wasn't about the conversation. Together they were coloring; together they were playing. The two seemed in perfect harmony as long as neither hogged the crayons. "What happened?" were among the first words of their conversation, as my son noticed a small burn or scrape on the other kid's arm. "A boo boo" was the answer and quickly he pointed at my son's noticeable arm covering. He had a "boo boo" as well.

That was it. That's all that was said, and back to coloring they went. The question didn't matter, and neither did the answer. They weren't pointing out the visible ailments to identify differences, but rather acknowledge similarities.

Neither noticed the challenges the other faced, but rather saw what they could accomplish together, a beautifully colored picture.

We can learn a lot from kids. Instead of taking time to stop and smell the roses, take time to stop and watch your children take in life. They don't notice the cast cover or other barriers us adults do. In fact, they look past what makes us different and focus on what makes us all the same. They see others for who they are, in their purest forms. They see new friends interested in coloring or racing down a water slide. Outside of anything adults may notice, all they see is a friend in the making.

Maybe if we focus on what connects us, we will spend less energy on what divides us. If we can stop rubbernecking and judging those around us, maybe we can start living life to its fullest. What would our world be like if we didn't allow ourselves to get bogged down by the things that could hold us back, and instead put energy into what will drive us forward? Embrace the vision of a child, prone to see individual goodness and unaware of identifying differences. "Boo boos" and cast covers aside, we are all alike at our core, just wanting to make meaningful connections.

CHAPTER 18
It's All About the Play-Doh

Sometimes short people get overlooked. I know because being short myself, unless I make a point to be heard, I can get lost in the background of a sea of tallness. I'm not the only one predisposed to getting unnoticed. The children among us are in a similar situation, and their inability to effectively communicate their thoughts doesn't help. Emotional outbursts mixed with a limited vocabulary makes them not only hard to interpret but less likely to be taken seriously. In my experience, I'd say it's their jumbled words that have the most meaning.

At the age of three, my son didn't let his height stop him from interjecting his thoughts. In fact, he said lots of things, many of which I would just laugh off. "Momma, will you help me go potty?" "Momma, you need to fix your hair. It looks crazy when you get out of the shower." "Momma, I have a baby in my belly, too, like you." At this age, I loved his voice and the way he said words or struggled to say some of them. I loved everything about him, but what I really loved most was his outlook on life.

One of his most consistent words was "outside" and that summer he would do anything for a few extra minutes in the yard to play with rocks or walk around the neighborhood and look for water meters (yes, really — he liked to find the gray metal meters in front of houses!). Outside to me wasn't nearly as exciting as I tend to melt in the summer's heat and bugs have always been most attracted to me. To me, "outside" was a hazardous zone. But my son saw it for what it was — God's gift to us.

One evening, we were drawing on the driveway with chalk when we came upon a trail of ants. I contemplated calling pest control, but my son was mesmerized. He would watch each as they meandered into our drawing area, inquisitive on where it was heading. I was seeking any moment to eliminate them, and when I thought he wasn't looking, squashed a persistent one with my hand. I didn't think anything of it until I noticed that trail of ants we had just watched traverse through the chalk were no longer moving and my son's hand was covered in the beautifully colored powder. He had watched me eliminate my distraction, and he started doing the same by squashing them, too.

In the midst of him enjoying God's creation, I had inadvertently encouraged him to destroy it.

While he found it a fun game, my heart sank, realizing I had taken away his joy, and possibly God's.

Once winter hit, my son gravitated to working with Play-Doh as the activity of choice. He loved to watch me roll the colorful substance into shapes or make spaghetti for a make-believe dinner. Play-Doh was special, so when he had an extra good day, we brought it out and celebrated. My son was picky about who he would allow to play it with him. My dad and I (P-Paw as my son named him) were among the only two who could.

After a rough work week mixed with full-fledged pregnancy hormones, I was a recipe for disaster, and a date night was much needed. My dad stayed over that night to get my son to bed and allow us a little extra time out, with plans to help us get ready for church the following morning. When he signed up to babysit, he didn't know that also came with some ongoing venting from yours truly. Lucky him, I had a new set of ears to hear my woes.

As we walked to the car the following morning to head to church, my son wouldn't stop talking. The problem was, I wasn't listening; I was still telling his P-Paw my woes. I helped my son climb into his car seat, while not skipping a beat on telling my story to my dad. I even asked my jabbering toddler to hang on as I finished what I needed to say but to no avail. I buckled him in and, as P-Paw leaned in to give him a goodbye kiss, I took a breath in between my thoughts and that was when my heart broke. I finally heard what my mini-me had been trying to say through his stuttered vocabulary.

I summoned my dad, who had already made his way to leave, back to listen to what his grandson was saying. "P-Paw, will you come play Play-Doh with me again?" A simple sentence with such meaning, such purpose, such yearning and passion and love. A simple sentence to many that would be overlooked — and one I had overlooked and still may have if I hadn't been open to listening.

For one second, humor me and throw away all that you know as an adult. Forget that Play-Doh is probably over-priced and not that interesting. Forget that we have cars and electronics and bills and money. Forget everything that we think matters and for a minute, try to look at life from the eyes of a kid.

Kids don't understand money — in fact, the littlest among them think five pennies are worth more than one dollar. Kids don't see differences in people — except maybe the boo-boo on your knee that you need a momma to kiss and make better. Kids don't value materials.

You don't see them comparing their motorized car with their neighbor's tricycle. No, they don't have that lens in life.

Instead, they get excited when they get to go outside and run in the sprinkler. They look forward to seeing their friends and have grins from ear to ear when they get to eat marshmallows (my son's favorite treat at that age). They look forward to bath time and coloring pages. They love it when you hold their hands and swing them in the air, and when you tickle them and can't stop laughing. They are happy when you are happy and, really, they just want to make you happy. They love it when people spend time with them, and especially when that time is spent playing Play-Doh.

When my son said that one sentence, I realized that the stress in my life didn't matter or at least it shouldn't. What matters most is spending time with those I love, and especially the "short" ones … my kids. In just a few words, my son put life in perspective. Our kids have so much to teach the world each and every day. The question isn't so much what is it they are going to say, it's more are we open to listening?

Listening is an active process. You have to physically and deliberately toss out the noise in your life to hear the little nuggets of truth that are all around you. Are you willing to do that? Why is that so hard? Is it that our world is moving a mile a minute? Maybe you can make the case for that excuse? I tend to think it's easier to squash the ant and the distractions around you than it is to observe glimpses of God's beauty for all they are worth. It's easier to roll with the waves and not take deliberate action in your life. And sometimes that deliberate action is a simple one — like merely *listening*. When you open your ears to hear more than words, it's then you realize that it's all about the Play-Doh.

CHAPTER 19
The Essence of Magic

Find me a good book, and I could be amused for hours upon end. I love to read because a book has the power to teleport me into make-believe. Going to the movies gives me that false sense of reality, too. Whether it's action-packed or a comedic romance, I love diving into the thickening of a plot. I grew up doing theater, so if I find the time to watch a play, my heart, too, is warmed.

I'm not alone in some of my favorite pastimes as many people also enjoy these activities. And why wouldn't someone enjoy these pursuits? They fill your mind with new thoughts and experiences while providing you time away from reality. Where I differ, however, is the fact that I don't allow myself the opportunity to take in the full capacity of each reading or viewing. You see, before I sit down to read a book, I skip to the end and read it first. Before I watch a movie, I research the conclusion, so I can be prepared. As a child theater guru, I can't help but analyze the quality of each actor during any theatrical performance.

I can't take a movie for face-value or give a book its fullest potential. Instead, I have to know the ending before I even meet the key players. I have to look for the flaws in the production or question the quality of the theatrical skills. While I still thoroughly enjoy these experiences in my own way, I have come to realize my approach requires a little preparation and a bit less magic.

What is magic anyway? As a kid, I got a magic set for Christmas. I guess I thought that set came with fairy dust and an invisible cloak because when I found the instructions to learn sleight of hand, I rethought my magician aspiration. Speaking of Christmas, I wasn't surprised to learn that the jolly ol' man you can find at every shopping center each year is just a guy, like you and me, trying to make some cash so he can indulge in the expectations brought by the holidays.

Before having kids, I entertained the thought of not celebrating holidays that used make-believe characters. No Santa or the Tooth Fairy. No Easter Bunny. But by power of suggestion, I opted to follow tradition, and now I am glad I did.

Remember that trip we took to Disney World, complete with a plaster cast? Well, that trip was about magic too. Our family of five really deserved a vacation, as we had never been on one together. Some thought we were crazy to make the trek, but we were determined to go. If I was being honest, deep down I actually thought we were crazy, too. But it was promised to be an experience of a lifetime, right? And a magical experience at that.

If I learned anything from the trip, I realized that my definition of magic was skewed. I thought it was making the impossible possible; turning nothing into something and something into nothing. I thought it was rabbit-hat pulling tricks or disappearing acts. No one told me there was more to magic than that. But there is, and I saw it first-hand.

Magic isn't the unseen; no, it's totally seen. It's not invisible; in fact, it's completely visible. It's not impossible; it's totally possible and readily available.

I found it the moment we had lunch with our favorite Disney characters. I found it when the world-renowned Mickey Mouse locked eyes with my kids and approached our family. I was almost robbed of the magic when I remembered that behind the suit was a person merely making a living. But I realized that the magic doesn't live in the costume or the autographing; the magic was in the eyes of my son.

They glistened in a way I'd never seen. His smile enlarged to a width was that unprecedented. I could see every muscle in his body tense up as Mickey neared, unsure if he should leap out of the chair or be shy because he was meeting THE Mickey. Then Minnie Mouse made her grand entrance. My daughter was smitten as Minnie leaned down and kissed her on her forehead. I've given her countless kisses, but this one was uniquely special. Those few minutes that were shared with each character were moments you can't prepare for. You can have your camera ready and your autograph book open, but the magic is uncharted territory.

The rest of our trip involved more experiences much like our first "character encounters." As we met each, my kids' magic tanks grew. My son had a skip to his step as he scouted character sightings for us to meet, hug and get signatures from. My daughter, holding her princess wand tight, waited patiently for each.

Those moments confirmed why I would never rob my kids of Santa or their belief in any other beloved character. The realities of life are hard, and our world can be tainted in many ways. They deserve some magic in their lives. I wanted them to believe in the make-believe and understand what is possible when we think life seems impossible. I wanted them to realize, one day they will be able to make magic by gifting it to another.

My worry that believing in make-believe would set the stage for disbelief in real topics that are hard to understand, such as God, just isn't true. While we worked to instill a strong belief system in our kids at a young age, their minds still struggled to comprehend what most of us adults continue to grapple with. I realized that Mickey Mouse and his friends were instead building upon a foundation we had set. They helped my kids see that something that seemed unattainable could be reached and touched and hugged. He was worth believing in as he was real in every kid-sense of a way. Believing implanted a sense of wonder as they were awe-struck, and I couldn't help but feel that this opportunity to believe in something you could see would help my kids continue to believe in that which is harder to see.

My kids and I experienced magic differently on this trip. The magic that engulfed Mickey's castle I could see through and poke holes at. But one thing I couldn't find flaws in was the magic that was implanted within my kids.

I owe it to my kids and myself to care less about how a book will end and enjoy the plot as it unfolds.

I learn from them how to stop analyzing the how and start believing the why. The journey is so much more than the conclusion. Critical questioning can be a distraction that could prevent you from living life to its fullest. It definitely doesn't let you live life magically.

Magic is all around you — from the people you meet to the experiences you encounter. God purposefully positions these magical moments in your life, but it's your responsibility to be open to them. Toss away what you think you know. Stop living from your mind and live with your heart. Find your fairy dust and pull out your princess wand, and if you don't see the magic, make it for others. That's your charge in this world — bringing happiness to others above yourself. If you do so, you won't be disappointed. In fact, you will be fulfilled in ways you never thought possible. Maybe then, you will be able to fully experience the pure essence of magic!

CHAPTER 20

Be the Reason

Each of us has a purpose. Some say God broke the mold when He made them, and I agree but for a different reason than you may think. I believe that we are unique in many ways, including our purpose. The day my son was born, it was apparent to me that God placed him here for a distinctive reason and his purpose was predestined. I knew my life would be made better with him in it, but I wasn't prepared for how others' lives would change, too.

I was once told that what you feed your soul is what you will reap. So, we made church a priority in our lives, hoping to feed our kids a life of faith so they would grow up knowing God's house was their home. We attended weekly mass and participated in church activities such as the annual picnic and Vacation Bible School. But my favorite annual tradition has always been a Lenten ritual.

Every Lenten season, my dad and I convene on Fridays at church and participate in the Stations of the Cross. While most people *give something up* for Lent each year, at a young age, I always *took something on* with my dad. Omitting a chocolate addiction is a perfect sacrifice for some, but I always offer a sacrifice of my time while replenishing my soul. As a kid, when my friends would schedule Friday rendezvous, during this season, I would be found at church praying. I would be lying to myself if I didn't admit that this was a tough sacrifice to be consistent with, but we always went. And while we were among the youngest in the sparse collection of die-hard Catholics, our tradition made me comfortable in God's house.

All I wanted was for my firstborn to experience this tradition. So, when Lent arrived that first year, he joined me, sleeping soundly in his car seat for the duration of the dedicated prayer time. As the next year came, I was excited for my sweet little boy to experience Stations of the Cross by learning the ritualistic movements — stand, sit, genuflect, repeat — which was wishful thinking.

At 15 months, sitting still in one place for any period of time was unrealistic. My expectation of being able to actually follow our deacon as he walked us through Jesus' stations is comical now. Instead, I spent that Friday trying to hold him back from distracting anyone else. I occupied my son with snacks and books while everyone else prayed. I tried to pray, but my prayer was as simple as "God, please keep him from yelling at the top of his lungs."

No amount of silence is good with a kid that age, so when I found myself deep in prayer without him making a peep, I realized he was too quiet for comfort. A quick glance proved I was right. He had leaned forward to distract an elderly lady who was kneeling and praying behind us. He got her attention by squatting down to get in her line of sight, and once he did, he had made a connection. He smiled one of his dimply smiles directly at her, and he didn't stop. I was mortified until I saw something beautiful happen. The woman who was praying so intently smiled back. I uttered apologies, but she wouldn't accept them as that single moment filled her with more joy than she had probably expected that evening.

From that point on, church became a place where I realized God would work wonders through my son. As my son grew, so did his collection of moments where he left a lasting impression on others in our congregation, including our priest.

If you were to have asked my son what his favorite part of church was, for years he would've told you Communion time. I loved that part of Mass, too, but for much different reasons. To him, this was his chance to get as close as possible to our priest for a special blessing. Our priest was his direct line to God, and he was always prepared to use that connection when he needed to.

One weekend, my son was antsy to go to Communion. I took it as a positive move in his faith, but his eagerness was for a whole different reason. That weekend was an extra memorable one as much he had just started to get the hang of potty training. During Mass, he had successfully put his newfound skills to work. We made a big to do about it — providing as much positive reinforcement as we could in such a quiet setting. We were proud; my son was beaming.

As we lined up to receive Communion, I could see the sheer joy that he had on his face about his recent accomplishment. I approached Father, bowed my head and accepted the Body of Christ. As I walked away, I glanced back as my son was in line to receive his blessing. Father placed his hand on my son's head and then unexpectedly leaned in to listen to my son tell him a story.

My face turned red, and so did my husband's. The only acceptable word spoken during Communion is "Amen," and there I watched my son hold up the line to tell Father much more than that. When we arrived back to our safe haven, the "cry room," my husband shared the magnitude of the experience that had unfolded. Apparently, my son was talking up a storm, and my husband persistently asked that he keep quiet. But when my son reached Father and looked him right in his eyes, a smile that painted his entire face proudly proclaimed that he went poop on Father's potty!

What's a priest to do when he's only used to people saying "Amen"? Well, Father smiled back, patted him on the head after giving him his blessing and congratulated him on his accomplishment!

I wish I could say that this was the only time that my son has had a conversation with our priest during Communion, but this experience was the first of many. When Father would wear a new robe, my son would point it out to him. Father grew a beard, and my son acknowledged it. A box sat next to the alter collecting canned goods for those in need, and my son exclaimed loudly to Father that it was wrapped in Star Wars paper. Each experience embarrassed me, but the one I giggle most about now is the time my son looked up at Father during Communion, and instead of saying a word, he put his fingers in his mouth, pulled out his cheeks and made a silly face right at our priest. As always, Father smiled and patted him on his head.

I'm sure others in the congregation may have shaken their heads and judged us as parents. I would have then if I had been in their shoes, but not today. Now, after years of unpredictability, my perception of church has changed quite a bit.

Next time you're in God's house — look around. Who do you see? Close your eyes. What do you hear?

You'll see Father preaching from the altar. You'll hear God's Word through the readings and homily. But look harder and listen more deeply. God's presence is all around in each and every person there. Whether or not you follow the rules of engagement, I've learned that isn't what matters most.

What matters is that no matter what, God is the center of our world.

To my son, church is home, and our priest is how he can talk to God. He knows that in God's house, anything is possible. Through his actions — be they acceptable or not — he shows others just how easy it is to feel His presence. With that in mind, why wouldn't my son have been excited to share with Father his potty training achievement? Why wouldn't he be ecstatic to know that God loves Star Wars as much as he does? Of course, through that lens, it all makes sense.

One weekend at church we were on our way to Communion, and while carrying my daughter, I tensed up as my son tugged on her leg to get her attention. My husband tried to hold back anything that was going to come out of his mouth, knowing of his repeat offenses. But instead, something beautiful happened. My daughter gazed at her brother, and he put his hand to his mouth, blew her a kiss and proceeded to whisper, "I love you." To my amazement, she repeated the behavior back. Without saying a word, my husband and I knew that all of our energy was well worth it.

God works through each of us daily in big ways and in small ones. He works through those we love and through those whose lives we barely come into contact with. It could be through the smile of a sweet little boy or one of their random outbursts. Sometimes we know that we've touched the life of another and other times we have no clue. That's the beauty of life, and it confirms that we should never hold back.

We shouldn't live in a world confined by societal rules and norms. Break out of the box. Be yourself. Give love and, I promise you, you will receive it back tenfold.

God made you to be you for a reason. Be that reason. You never know who you may inspire — or even make laugh — in the process.

SECTION 5

THE POWER OF ONE

Strength in numbers may be important at times, but never underestimate the power of one. One small gesture, one phone call, one hug … One person has the incredible ability to turn the light back on in another's life. Our impact can never be measured, for it is like ripples in a pond when a stone is tossed. Each toss promises not to leave the water still. Some make quiet ripples and others large waves, but each extends far beyond its original intent. Toss yourself out there. Every time you do, you have promised to leave a legacy.

Your Story Matters

A Good Deed Doesn't Go Unnoticed

Best Friends

Finding Angels

Believe in Humanity

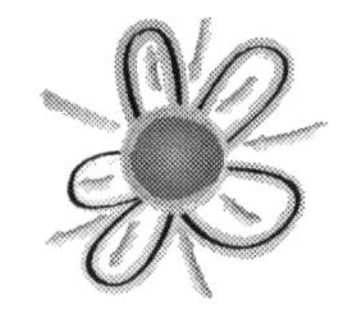

CHAPTER 21
Your Story Matters

I may be an outgoing, up-for-anything kind of person for most of the day, but when it's time to recharge, I can become a recluse with the best of them. It's not just that I enjoy quiet time, but after hours of being "on," when it's time to be "off," my switch can get stuck to the point where I actually panic when the phone rings or someone knocks at my door.

When I inadvertently pass an acquaintance at the grocery store, I try to navigate down a neighboring aisle so as to avoid a conversation. It's not that I'm anti-social, but it's that prepping for extroversion requires some time to give my face muscles rest and relaxation.

As with any hibernation, a premature jolt back to reality catches me off guard, and my "A" game tends to be taken down a notch to more like a "B" or "C" scrimmage. So, when I met him on the sidewalk as I was in my secluded fog, meandering to gather the mail, I had to internally slap myself on the face to wake up, be "on" and be present.

Our neighborhood is a quiet one, which is what we love most about living outside the city. We can count the stars each night, wildlife is abundant, and most of my neighbors keep to themselves, but a few have regular dates with their dogs and the sidewalk.

The day was beautiful for November. It was unseasonably warm, and the gorgeous array of fall colors made it feel like I was living in a Bob Ross painting with his "happy little trees." I had just returned home when I saw a package in the mailbox, so even though my body yearned to be inside with the blinds drawn, I opted to get the mail.

He was walking down the sidewalk in front of my house at the same time that I reached my destination. By the time I saw him there was no hiding from the inevitable. I was going to have to engage in a friendly conversation. I smiled at my neighbor and said what every "nice-but-I-don't-want-to-talk" person says, "Beautiful day isn't it?" Instead of mumbling a short, one-word answer and continuing on, he turned his gaze to me and started a deep dialogue.

I would have been all right with a little friendly chat, but the conversation evolved into complicated topics such as global warming and ended with more details than I care to recall about his digestive struggles and a recent surgery he'd had to rectify those troubles. I kept scooting back closer to my house, trying to give the non-verbal cues that it was time to wrap up the conversation, but he continued anyway.

Right before I mentally told myself I had had enough, he shared that while he had been through a lot, he could never complain. He was grateful for miracle workers in his life, and his doctor was one. He had given him a way to live again through his surgery. So, he was going to celebrate that he could walk around the neighborhood and live life more comfortably thanks to all that his doctor had done for him.

I paused and smiled as I realized who this neighbor was. I had met him at Halloween that year as I took my kids door-to-door collecting more sweets than their buckets and bellies could handle. I recalled our interaction with him because that night he had gone out of his way to talk to my littles about their costumes in great depth, teetering into lengthy conversation as well.

As I stood there listening to his story, I was filled with gratitude for the sweet conversations he had had with my family just the month prior. At that time, he focused on my children, but this time, it was my turn to hear his story, and I realized that his story had even more pages than I would have thought.

Don't all of ours? Aren't we all hiding behind a mask of make-up and make-believe most days, answering the most basic of questions with the most basic of answers?

> *"Good morning. How are you doing today?"*
>
> *"Fine."*

But we aren't really fine, are we? We may be ecstatic, literally about to jump out of our own skin with excitement around some news we just heard. Or maybe we are livid at even being asked the question before we can get our daily dose of caffeine down. Or maybe something may be weighing heavy on our hearts, and just waking up that day is an accomplishment. Whatever the case, "fine" is never the true answer, is it?

I don't know my neighbor's full story, except for the unexpected excerpts he shared that day, but I do know that he lives his life outside himself, not hiding behind his worries or thoughts. He doesn't stop and question what others think before he shares, and sometimes overshares! He takes each question at face value, accepting that his converser wants a real answer, not a sugar-coated, meaningless "fine." He doesn't let himself stand in his own way, and he praises goodness every time he sees it, no matter who he sees it through.

I have so much to learn. Like how I should always have five minutes to spare to talk to someone who actually wants to converse. I shouldn't dodge someone I know in the grocery store just because I didn't put on my makeup that day. I need to start answering the phone, not sending it to voicemail, and I have to stop hiding when the doorbell rings unless it's at an odd hour when no one in their right mind should be out trying to make conversations. (Then, hiding may be warranted!)

I don't know my neighbor's side of our encounter, but I trust our short interaction left him as uplifted as it did me. I'm hopeful that he ran into others like me on his stroll, originally dodging human interaction, and he spoke to them anyway. I hope he left a nugget of his life with them and that he continues to do it everywhere he goes.

We don't know the title of everyone's life book or what's written on each page. We don't know their underlying themes or where their plot thickens. We don't have to know any of the twists or turns, but what we do know is their story matters and so does ours.

In fact, it matters enough to be shared and to be heard. Don't hoard your story or allow it to collect dust. Don't close your book and hide beneath the hardback. Be like my neighbor, an open book, and share a piece of you with all whom you meet whether others care to listen or not because they may need to hear exactly what you have to say at that exact moment. Your words or the word of another could leave a lasting impression, shaping your story as you author the book of your life.

CHAPTER 22

A Good Deed Doesn't Go Unnoticed

I was pregnant—like really pregnant! My ankles were swollen, and walking was something I did only if it was absolutely necessary to get from point A to point B. I was nearing the end of my pregnancy and, after delivering two babies, I knew that as much as I didn't want to walk, it was the only way to evict our family's newest addition from its comfy warm-womb residence. So, I decided to go shopping.

My mom and I explored the store and then made our way to the checkout line. The line was short, thank goodness, as I was already calculating the minutes it would take until I could plop my unusually round body down in the car to rest.

We were up next when an elderly couple got in line behind us. Noticing that they only had a few items, my mom offered to let them proceed in front of us. I don't have a poker face, so unfortunately, my expression was, I am sure, completely on point with how I was feeling.

I was fuming. Here I was, about to literally pop, and my mom let someone go in front of us. I couldn't see why it was so critical that at that time on this day with my current condition, she felt the need to put others before ourselves. Couldn't she see I was teetering on exhaustion?

Why had she decided that the couple behind us was more important than me? After the couple saw my condition, why didn't they turn down my mom's offer? Instead, the couple smiled and eagerly jumped in front of us in line and continued to the checkout lane.

I wish that I could say their order went smoothly, but that was far from the truth. In fact, the couple questioned every price that rang on the register, causing the clerk to call for backup and adjustments to be made. The couple even looked back at us and made the comment "I bet you're wishing you didn't offer to let us go before you." It took everything out of me to not lose it.

A few weeks later, the walking paid off and we welcomed a little boy into our family! I loved every baby cuddle, but it didn't take long after his birth for me to itch for an outing. My husband and I packed up all three kiddos, and we trekked back to the same store for the first time as a family of five.

To keep my older two kids happy, we typically bribed them with a soft pretzel and a blue Icee during the shopping adventure. That day, I tasked my husband to take the older two to get their usual, and the baby and I went another direction to pick up some necessities.

I had been gone one minute when I identified the tone of my daughter's shrieks from across the store. I had just felt a moment of pride that my husband and I made this "parenting of three" thing look good when I heard the meltdown and saw the dilemma. My husband knew that both kids would be completely sugar-ridden if each got an Icee, so he had opted for them to share one. The problem was my daughter had other plans, and my oldest son was not in the sharing mood.

People cast judgment as was evidenced by the stares we received from every direction. I flooded my husband's ears with discontent, questioning his decisions that led to pure chaos. My confidence in our parenting skills faltered. As we turned to walk to the produce section, the clerk from the concession stand came running our way with another large Icee in hand. She handed it to my daughter, smiled and jetted back to her register.

I've worked in food establishments before, so I know that most companies only care about the bottom line. To keep a positive work situation, the clerk probably paid for that Icee out of her own pocket. But that didn't stop her. She saw a situation and knew she had the opportunity to help out. And she did as my daughter's tears stopped immediately and that little squirt drank every bit of her drink.

After we finished shopping and loaded the car, we remembered we'd forgotten an item on our list, so I ran back in to purchase it. As I approached the scanner at the self-checkout lane, I realized I'd accidentally cut the line. A man was originally in front of me, so I encouraged him to complete his purchase first, apologizing for my oversight. He insisted that I go ahead of him which I am sure he later regretted. I tried to scan my membership card, but it wouldn't work. I tried to scan my items, but they, too, wouldn't scan.

I turned around and asked the man if he had any tips for working the kiosk. He impatiently took my card and proceeded to literally scan my items, my membership card and even my credit card because I was proving incompetent. As I thanked him profusely, I said: "I guess you probably regretted letting me go in front of you."

The words rolled out of my mouth so fast that I couldn't stop them. Immediately, I was taken back to the experience with my mom a few weeks prior. This time, instead of being the impatient one, I was the grateful one. Instead of being frustrated at those around me, I was thankful for those who helped me when I needed them. This time, I had more context — I knew what my day was like. I knew how the small gesture of going first made a difference to me. I knew that I really appreciated this man's help. I knew all of this, but this man did not. He knew nothing about my situation — and I am sure that he was frustrated with me like I was the elderly couple. How many times in life do we get the chance to see life from both angles?

Maybe some days we are the one with the extra pennies that we give the coffee barista after purchasing our beverage and some days we are the person that is a penny short and are grateful for the spare change. Some days we are the ones with a little time on our hands and open to allowing that one car that went against the driving rules to merge in front of us and other times we are the ones illegally using the emergency lane to frantically get to our destination.

We typically live so consumed with our own thoughts and feelings we forget that we are merely one person in a sea of many. Our one person, though, is extremely powerful and we have the potential to change the world around us if we opt to look outside ourselves.

Months later, my family visited the same store again and, like always, we went to get the kids a pretzel and two Icees. My husband muttered under his breath that the lady taking our order was probably rolling her eyes that we were back, but glad we'd learned our lesson and bought two drinks. When I realized she was indeed the same lady who had come to our saving grace, I got her attention, determined to tell her our story of being a new family of five saved by her act of kindness. I teared up as I thanked her. She was surprised and shared that she, too, has been in our shoes and wanted to help in whatever way she could.

Angels come into our lives daily. Sometimes you see them. Sometimes they run, drop off a blue Icee and leave. Sometimes, you are the angel and yet you may never know if you happened to be the glue to holding together another person that day. Whether you are the angel or are impacted by an earthly angel, one thing is certain. To Him, a good deed doesn't go unnoticed.

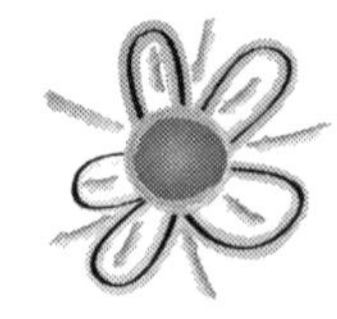

CHAPTER 23

Best Friends

We've all succumbed to those eye-catching quizzes that pop up on our social media newsfeeds and lure us in to wasting about 10 minutes of your life that you are promised to never get back. I'm a sucker for a good one that tells me which Disney character I most emulate or what Hollywood star is my doppelganger.

As an OCD gal at her finest, I love lists, so make it a top 10 and I'm sold, especially if it helps me confirm what I already know — like "you're a millennial if ..." or "you know you're an only child when ..." One of my favorite online quizzes helps me reminiscence about my childhood when it validates that yes, I am indeed an 80s kid. But I already knew that because my doppelganger is "Punky Brewster" and "The Little Mermaid" was my childhood Disney movie of choice.

Besides the fact that my birth certificate endorses this truth, it would take one glance at a childhood photo with my bangs nearly touching the ceiling to never question the decade I came from. Well, that and the best friend necklace that was my prized possession.

I don't remember the moment or the day ... but I know the feeling that I had — because I can still feel it — when I met my best friend. She was a year older than me, but we liked the same things, like digging in the dirt to find hidden treasures and "rescuing" dead animals off the sides of roads to give them a proper burial. We were best friends, and we even had the heart-shaped puzzle necklaces to prove it.

We laughed. We danced. We rode horses and drew pictures. I was safe when I started kindergarten in a new school surrounded by new people because I had her. She always had my back, especially when she knew that holding my hand when we walked to the bus made me feel better. It didn't matter if the big kids made fun of us; it didn't stop her from being what she knew I needed right at that moment.

For years I prayed to be extra smart so that I could skip a grade and be in class with her. With that not being a reality, I was extra grateful for our time together after school and on the weekends. We did Girl Scouts together and even when I applied for my first job, she was there, working at the same movie theater and watching over me.

One winter night, I found myself reminiscing about my childhood days while I cuddled on the couch with my two oldest kids. I asked my son who he played with at school, and as he ran down the list of all of his friends, he made a point to acknowledge that while he loved playing with those kids, a few were his best buddies.

I asked my daughter next who her best friends were, but she shrugged and mumbled no one. Now, while I am confident that she did indeed play with kids in her class and loved every second of it, I see so much of myself in her shy soul. Not only is she a physical replica of me — from my dark attributes to my nervous hair-twirling — she tends to observe the world in a way I did at a young age when I waited for that moment of connection that would keep me safe and give my day meaning.

I asked her the question again, but she put her head down while diverting eye contact. I lifted her chin, so she would look at me and asked her what every mother should ask her daughter: "Sweet girl, can I be your best friend?"

Her eyes twinkled, and her mouth spread to a beautiful smile. After a theatrical "yes," she scooted closer to me on the couch ... as close as our bodies could get ... and she put her opened hand in my lap for me to hold. She then took her other hand and cupped it by her mouth, so she could whisper sweet nothings in my ear, and she proceeded to say, as if it was on repeat, "Momma, we're best friends."

My oldest son just laughed at it. "Momma, we're family. Of course, we're all best friends." He's right. That comes with the territory.

But sometimes as important as it is to say "I love you" to your family, it's equally as important for them to know that you are best friends forever.

Nothing can break that friendship. It's as solid as the corroded best friend necklace I have stashed in my memory box that my childhood friend and I wore for years. It may be tarnished and could use a little cleaning, but what relationship doesn't need that, right? In fact, doesn't every friendship require TLC? But lasting friendships don't get thrown away in the garbage. They linger and can be picked up at any point in life. True friendships are those that require the extra "F" on "BFF," those where no words are needed to keep you connected.

My best friend and I grew up and grew apart. She moved, and we both now have families with kids of our own. Our paths rarely cross, but our hearts will forever be intertwined. Thank you, my dear friend, for showing me what a best friend is made of. She left me with big shoes to fill, but

I pray that I can be at least half the best friend she was to me for my sweet daughter and the rest of my children. I know it won't be easy, but for now, I do what every good best friend does. I giggle and paint toenails and cuddle close while we sneak a piece of candy and whisper gossip in each other ears.

Everyone deserves to have a relationship like this in their lives. Maybe it's your childhood friend or your spouse. Maybe it's your parent or your child. Maybe it's your faith — talk about a relationship that is always waiting for us no matter where we are, who we've become or what we have heavy on our hearts. Wherever you find it, cherish it for we are meant to be connected. We are meant to not hide and be true to ourselves. We are meant to hold hands and be a safe place for another.

When you find your one person, cherish them and that connection, and make a promise to pay it forward.

My best friend paved the way to help me become one, and my sweet daughter of mine, please don't worry. Your momma will always be yours.

CHAPTER 24
Finding Angels

Our bags were packed, and two of my three kids were jumping inside our no-longer spacious van counting down the hours until we left. Not only had the day arrived that we were to embark on our journey to vacation, but the hour and minute had, too. After gathering a few final necessities, taking a quick restroom break and strapping the kids in their seats, we were set to leave on time, a rarity for us.

As I dragged the last item to the van, several things seemed out of sorts. My youngest was crying as he tried to crawl into the vehicle while the older two stared at him perplexed, and there wasn't an adult in sight. My mom had been with us helping to get everyone ready for our trip, and my husband was normally no more than arms-length away from a kid at any moment. As I searched to find either, I noticed a stranger running up the driveway asking if she could assist in calling for help.

In moments like this, time literally stops. Panic set in as the woman veered to connect with my husband, who I spotted as I inched around the house from the garage. My husband was only a few feet away crouched on the sidewalk, and when our eyes met, I saw something in his that I have never seen before. He, too, was panicked, but for a whole different reason.

My mom was lying flat on the pavement. My husband was calling her name and, while I could tell that fear wasn't only consuming me, he kept his tone calming but fear was consuming him, too. My life seemed to stop as if Father Time had pressed the pause button on my life clock as I accepted that for a brief moment my mom was unconscious and unresponsive.

My kids jolted me back to reality as the onslaught of questions began, as if they were immune to the trauma unfolding merely feet away.

"Why aren't we leaving?" "Why is Mimi laying there?" For once, I didn't have answers. I had more questions.

During all this time, this stranger stayed with me. She knew what to do when I didn't. This woman whom I had never met didn't leave our sides. She pulled out her phone and called for help. She held my youngest, so I could attempt to help my daughter inside the house to use the bathroom. She played with my kids as we tried to keep Mom awake and aware. She let me cry to her when I ran out of words. She let me be terrified. That evening, my neighbor put on her walking shoes for some brisk exercise around the neighborhood but never dreamt that would entail being the glue for my family.

As the ambulance made its way to my house and my kids were corralled inside watching a show, I grabbed her and held her close. I buried my head in her shoulder and through the sobs I thanked her for her big heart and for being just what we needed when we needed it. I told her she was our angel, and I asked as she unwillingly left to finish her walk that she pray for my mom.

Four years prior, I had found myself in a similar conundrum. I had been in a rush to get to work early that day and decided to take my breakfast on the road. I'm a multitasker, and that morning I was testing my skills to their fullest. I was driving down our windy country roads glistening from the recent downpour while talking on the phone and eating yogurt from a cup. A recipe for disaster, I now know.

I looked down for a second to get a scoop of yogurt and when my eyes made contact again with the road, I overcorrected once I'd realized I had strayed too far to the right. I hydroplaned, and my car plummeted off the left side of the road, straight down a 15-foot drop-off deep within wooden terrain.

Again, I learned what it felt like for time to stop. I was unsure what to do, especially when I opened my door and couldn't figure out how to climb back up to the road. I felt lost, literally.

Then I saw them … two sets of hands followed by the voices of two earthly angels yelling down at me directions on how to climb out. I inched my way up to safety with their help but where I wrecked was anything but safe. I was between a blind spot and a hairpin curve, yet somehow the normally sparse road had two cars that had witnessed the experience, and two willing individuals who put their own lives on the line to save mine.

I don't remember who they were, but when I close my eyes, I remember how they made me feel. I was panicking and was stressed to the max, yet these two women held me close and fed me thankful thoughts. They were thankful that they had been there to see me swerve off the road because if they weren't no one would have found me. They were thankful that I hadn't veered off the road a foot more in either direction and struck a tree. They were thankful there was no on-coming traffic. They were thankful I was alive.

They stayed by my side and prayed with me. Not once did they lecture me for my poor behavior but rather lifted me up, realizing I was alive by the grace of God.

Like those fellow travelers on the side of the road, my neighbor was an angel. There is no doubt in my mind that is truth. Outside of the fact that she did so much for my family, I know she was an angel because when I asked her to pray, I believe in my heart she did, the moment she walked away, and didn't stop for several hours. I know this because her prayers worked. What could have been a tragic ending to an unfortunate situation wasn't. My mom only suffered some mild effects of a concussion and some expected bruising. Yes, we had a slight delay in our vacation travels, but I couldn't be more grateful that I still have my mom.

A few days after my wreck, I heard on the news that the exact same accident had occurred that very morning on another backcountry road in my town, except instead of dealing with a small scratch and some embarrassment, lives were taken too soon. I was able to walk away, and my car was still drivable, somehow with minimal damage. The "could haves" and "would haves" of my situation were just that, unnecessary worries, thanks to the prayers from the two unexpected angels that day.

Angels are all around us, you know. Sometimes we see them and remember their names or the smell of their perfume. Other times, we only remember the feelings they provoke from their brief time with us. They don't have visible wings or iridescent halos hovering. They come in all sizes — some with big tasks and others with small duties. Sometimes you don't know they are there until they are gone. But they are no doubt sent from God to help us through whatever predicament we have gotten ourselves in.

Sometimes, you are one and don't even know it. Had any of those people woken up that morning knowing they were meant to save someone? I venture to say, probably not. But when the time came, they listened to what God put in their hearts, and they made a difference in the life of another. Will you listen to what He puts in your heart? Will you allow Him to act through you and be an angel to another? Who knows, someone's life might depend on it.

CHAPTER 25

Believe in Humanity

Are we a country divided? Some would say there's no doubt. And during the week of a presidential election, all you have to do is check your social media newsfeed, and it will seemingly prove it. But one year when opinions were so polarizing, my trip to the polls may have proved this hypothesis wrong. In fact, that day, when I turned in my ballot and prayed for our country, I walked out of there with my head held high, my spirits lifted and my hope for humanity restored. Here's why.

I took up the challenge to exercise my civic duty and that year I traveled to the school where I was told I could place my vote. I knew that day would be emotionally charged for many, and as someone who is private with my political views, I prepped myself for what I was about to endure.

In most situations, I'm an extrovert. I always have an opinion and struggle not expressing it when I'm asked. But the one topic that is proven to silence this girl is politics.

When it comes to politics, I opt to live an introverted lifestyle, holding tight to my opinions and diverting controversial conversation; I do so because I have found it to be a lose-lose situation. Most times, I can wiggle out of politically charged chit-chat, but when the parking lot was packed early that morning, I knew that I wouldn't be able to avoid the inevitable, and I was right. While I could personally avoid verbal confrontation about my opinions, the hour-long wait to vote allowed me a front row seat to a discussion between strangers about their political viewpoints, of course from opposite ends of the spectrum.

An older couple stood patiently in line with smiles on their faces. A middle-aged and quite animated woman opened the conversation with them, first talking about trivial topics like the weather and voter turnout. But soon the conversation switched to typically heated topics in a place of no escape.

The woman behind me was a mother. She had a teenage son with her and a baby in a stroller. She was quiet at first, but any elongated wait will cause even the shyest person to let out a peep. She conversed with her son about the election, the right to vote and the importance of the day to our history.

I was sandwiched between the two conversations, and if I wanted to vote, I had no other option but to listen. The older couple was conservative, and the other woman was very liberal in her thinking. Their core viewpoints were different, so you would think that their conversation would be impassioned, but instead, these three were energized, not shying away from the discussion. In fact, I became mesmerized by the fact that while they didn't share the same politic beliefs, they respected each other.

Even though each topic ended with differing opinions, they constantly smiled and even laughed at times. There was no tension, and no one was trying to alter the viewpoint of another. They were who they were, and by the end of the wait, they would probably have voted for one another if their names were on the ballots.

The mother behind me was my hero that day. During such a challenging political season, I was relieved that I didn't have to explain anything about this mess to my kids. Agree with me or not, I want them to stay as naive as possible for as long as it makes sense. But this mom had no choice. While her son couldn't vote, it was time for her to help shape our future generation and talk about the importance of doing so. She spoke about the importance of the day and explained how companies were supposed to not stand in the way of allowing people their right to vote. She talked about how, no matter your viewpoint, it was critical to be there and do what so many people have fought for the right for.

My hour-long wait felt much shorter than it was, and I heard those around me acknowledge the same sentiments as we approached the voting stations. In fact, after the older couple signed their names on the dotted line and got their pieces of paper to make an impact on our country's history, the woman made eye contact with her new friend and gave her a hug. She grabbed her hand and thanked her for the conversation, noting she had thoroughly enjoyed it and they both agreed it made the time fly by.

I soaked it all in as I, too, signed my name, filled in the square boxes to place my votes and entered my ballot into the ballot-eating machine. After the five minutes it took to give my opinion, I took my "I voted" sticker to wear with pride, but for a reason that I never expected that day.

That morning I learned so much about those around us. I observed that not everyone who talks politics is polarizing or has a hidden agenda. I saw how differences don't always divide but can unite or not matter altogether. I watched a retired veteran slowly make his way into the gymnasium with his walker and was reminded, as I saw his caretaker support his every move, that our lives are bigger than any election. I'm not downplaying the topics that impact us all, but what I saw was how what truly impacts each of us is how we interact with one another.

We cast a vote, yet we may not really get to choose who leads our country. But we get to choose who leads us personally.

You have a choice each day you wake up and take in a deep breath of this God-given life how you're going to live it, who you are going to be and the difference you are going to make.

No one can choose that for you, and while others' decisions around you can leave lasting impressions, you get to choose how you process it all and what you put back into this world.

Among all the hatred, people bashing and foul behavior that that particular election week erupted, on Election Day I saw, more than ever, the power of humanity … and let me tell you, it wears red and blue equally. We can stand united, even with differing opinions and beliefs, as long as we don't let others divide us. It's our choice. If I'm choosing, I'm going to choose to be the mom who will one day teach my kids that we don't all have to be the same or think the same, but we do deserve respect all the same. I'm going to choose to love those who think differently from me, for they, too, are made from God. I'm going to choose, time and time again, love over hate, giving over receiving and to have hope even when it's hard to see.

I choose tackling this world together, for when we are a reflection of who we hope the world to be, we start to be the change. Stop attacking each other and leave judging for larger powers to be. Be love. Be respect. Be the difference.

SECTION 6

BE LOVE

There are a lot of things you can be. You can be tall or you can be short. You can be joyous or you can be saddened. Jealous or zealous. Kind or bitter. You can be passionate or passionless. Some things you can "be" you can't control, and others may just feel that way. But know this. God made you to be you, and when you live this way, all things fall into place. At the core of being you, all you have to be is love.

Love Her Heart

The Couple

Together

I Love You Too, Momma

A Garden of Love

CHAPTER 26
Love Her Heart

For those of you not from the South, some of our expressions may leave you puzzled. Like if we get really mad, we may inform you that we'll knock you into the middle of next week looking both ways for Sunday! Or if you ask how we are doing, we may leave you grossed out, explaining that we are hanging in there like a hair in a biscuit. That one always gets people but let's be honest; it makes a point! And ain't no one wanting to be so crazy busy that they are running around like a chicken with their head cut off ... especially this vegetarian!

While many of our phrases come from quite literal experiences, most times there just isn't any better way to get a point across. I tend to be a heart blesser, and unlike some of my fellow Southerners, I truly mean it when I say it. Others like to use the phrase when they are being facetious. Like when someone put on a poorly matched outfit. Bless their heart. Or that girl in church who doesn't realize that she definitely doesn't need to quit her day job and take up singing. Definitely bless her heart, too.

No, for me, I tend to heart bless when people really need it. When a tragedy hits or an extra prayer is warranted. Over the years, my blessings have evolved into loving. I can't quite put a finger on it as to when it happened, but I've become a heart lover. In fact, many know me by my "love your heart."

I mean it, though. When I meet someone whose heart is pure, I have to let them know that I love it. I feel fortunate because one of the purest of hearts lives under my roof and is the shyest of my bunch. But when that girl loves, she loves hard and with passion. My sweet daughter is the epitome of the phrase all bottled up into one pint-sized person.

It was the day after Thanksgiving. We'd hosted our families the day before, and while the food was delicious and the company even better, it still entailed planning and lots of cleaning. After a pleasant meal and an all-nighter of shopping, when the morning rolled around, I felt like I'd been run over by a freight train. But, it was a new day, and my three woke up bright-eyed and bushy-tailed. Lucky us.

With Thanksgiving behind us, it was time to focus on the next exciting event — Christmas. So, no matter how tired I was, it was time to put up the tree. I was just as excited to do it as the kiddos were so after my husband carried up the box and pieced it together, I was as happy as a tick on a fat dog to get to fluff the tree.

To keep the kids from barging in, I let them feel a branch and realize that it was prickly to the touch. Seeing all the scrapes on my hands was a constant reminder that the tree is for looking and not touching. They were all excited, no doubt about it. They couldn't wait to put on the ornaments, and all were in awe at the lights. But before any of those were visible, my daughter was thrilled just for the experience.

The tree was scrawny still, and there wasn't a star topper in sight, yet that sweet little girl repeatedly approached me as I was arms-deep trying to open all the branches. "Thank you, Momma," she told me and then she would find a place to hug me tight. At first, I questioned what I'd done to deserve that kind of gratitude. She hadn't found her stash of presents yet, and I hadn't given her an extra cookie. She was simply thankful for what was to come. For the tree and all that it meant to her.

Then a box arrived in the mail. In typical family fashion, we had forgotten that we ordered some things, so we all got excited, thinking it was a special gift. We all gathered around, only to realize that my daughter's birthday party decorations had arrived. With widened eyes, she scurried my way, wrapped her arms around my legs, and said, "Thank you, Momma."

A thankful spirit that soul has. Earlier that week, I picked her up early from school to take her to gymnastics. She was so excited, she literally did little bunny hops down the hall. She only paused to grab my hand and thank me. At dinner, when I gave her her favorite yogurt, she looked me in the eyes and thanked me, too. Even when we cuddled on the couch and shared a blanket, she thanked me.

While she is appreciative of gifts, it was the experiences that she was most grateful for. The tree didn't have to be beautifully decorated, but just the fact that I went through the trouble to put up the scrawny tree we had, she was happy. She didn't get upset if the snack I brought her after school wasn't what she was hoping for; she was grateful to have a snack. Her happy tank doesn't run out.

I can learn a lot from that sweet girl, and I venture to say all y'all can as well. She lives her life in the moment, and most days, she walks like she's on air. She's got a bounce in her step, a smile on her face and a twinkle in her eyes that can't be taught. I wish I could take ownership of it, but I feel confident God blessed us with her sweet soul just the way she is. She lights up the room and everyone she comes into contact with. I tend to think that her grateful heart and spirit make her light, as nothing holds her down. Her attitude is truly shaped by her gratitude.

Her teacher had shared that a week prior the students had been shuffled among classrooms because the Thanksgiving holiday meant fewer kids were there. So, my daughter was in a room with a different teacher. As her normal teacher passed my daughter in the hall, she yelled out for her, asking if she could give her a hug. Of course, who wouldn't want one?! And while the hug was special, no doubt, afterward, my daughter looked up at her teacher and thanked her for the hug back.

It's the little things, like a free pair of sunglasses or a hotel notepad that I would bring back from work trips. Or when I let her borrow one of my old necklaces to match her outfits. Sometimes it's just getting the chance to play with bubbles or chalk up the driveway. Or if I find an old shirt around the house with Minnie Mouse on it.

For her, it's not the stuff that she's most grateful for. It's the meaning behind it, and the experiences that are attached.

She realizes that the stuff most people are thankful for will break, wear and tear, and go out of style. What is worth it in life aren't things but experiences. It isn't fads but those around us who make us most happy. In her short years on Earth, she has embodied the true spirit of love and can teach us all what true love means. To this Southern girl, I think she's finer than frog hair split four ways. Yes, I do love her heart. One-hundred percent!

CHAPTER 27
The Couple

When I was a kid, I kept a clean bill of health. While that should be something worth celebrating, I always had a tinge of jealousy when a classmate would show up wearing a new pair of glasses. While the new spectacles would help them see the world with a new level of sharpness, I was more interested in how cute the new frames were and secretly bummed that I had perfect vision. In fact, I would occasionally cover each eye independently to check to see if I had any solid rationale to talk my mom into taking me to the eye doctor for a check. And one day I did!

Contacts and glasses lived up to the hype, but after a few decades, the newness wore off and the daily ritual of contact cleaning became a burden. Over time, I cut corners on removing my disposables until one day I paid the price.

You know the feeling you get when you get an eyelash lodged in your eye or a popcorn kernel burrowed in between your teeth? I become manic when that happens, pulling out the floss or rubbing my eye uncontrollably. The night previously I had accidentally slept in my contacts, so when I woke up and felt this discomfort even after taking them out, I knew that an eyelash had made its way in. I rubbed. I wiped. I flushed with saline solution and got a wet rag to scrub. I did everything except look in the mirror, and the moment that I resorted to the obvious, I had to pick my jaw up off the floor.

When I saw a white spot in the middle of my eye, I knew something wasn't right. After more removal attempts and a last resort call to the on-call eye doctor, I met a new arch nemesis. Stephanie, meet your cornea ulcer.

Who gets those?! Apparently, my name is now among the list of others who have had a careless moment with their contacts. And while the eye sore was less than visibly appealing, thank heavens it wasn't a smidgen lower, where it would have caused permanent vision loss.

An eye doctor appointment was warranted but when I pulled up to the parking lot that day I realized I wasn't alone in that need as evidenced by the lack of parking spaces. I drove around three times praying for someone to leave but instead parked in the business adjacent to my destination. I mustered up the strength to brave the elements as that day was one of the coldest that season and I made my way in to hear my eye's fate.

As I approached the front door, my body begged to get inside. I had to press the brakes as an elderly couple had the same goal in mind. They fit the description of a "sweet old couple" in every way. From the way she touched his shoulder as he inched forward out of the bitter cold maneuvering his walker to the nonverbal cues of two people who have been together longer than they have been apart. These two didn't move without the other, and it was obvious nothing would change that.

He was the patient, and she was taking him to the doctor. But while his ailments made it challenging for him to get to his destination, she too faced her own challenges. Her tremors were severe (I remember recognizing the symptoms as possibly the onset of Parkinson's), and they caused her to struggle at even holding open the door. I jumped in to do it for them, letting them both enter into the waiting room.

She motioned for him to find a place to sit while she signed him in, something seemingly easy yet daunting for her to accomplish. Her shaky hand caused her to struggle to stay within the sign-in lines as she tried to write his personal information, so the office knew of his arrival. What should have taken a minute or less took several. I was impatient and even asked the receptionist if there was another sign in sheet I should use but was informed that this woman had the only one. I didn't realize until later that me asking that question pressured her to try to move faster even though her body wouldn't allow it.

As she grabbed her seat after completing the necessary paperwork, I noticed a sigh in her breath so subtle as to not let her husband see the challenges that she faced for him. Instead, she mumbled to him, letting him know she had him taken care of, as always as I expect. I went to sign in, and as I saw her scribbled attempt on the sign-in sheet, I was livid with myself.

What was so important that I needed to gain an extra few seconds at this woman's expense? Yes, I was concerned about my eye situation, but for the moment I could see, albeit behind bulky glasses, but I could see nonetheless. After I signed in and found a chair to wait, I couldn't stop watching this couple. Even through my blurred vision, I saw a love that withstood the test of time.

She loved him, as he did her. To the point where nothing stood in the way of helping each other, not even their bodies beginning to fail them. They didn't ask for help, for all I know they didn't have any, but they huddled together in the brisk winter wind and made it to their appointment. Together. Each one needed the other. And together they navigated their life, one wobbly step at a time.

As I waited, I thought about my own life, grateful that I have found a love that will withstand all. As I watched them, I realized the importance, yet again, of the moment.

Time measured by a clock is a human invention, but time in God's hands is a collection of moments. Like the hands on a clock, moments fly by if you don't take time to savor them.

I frequently forget that time isn't something I own. It is a gift given, and it's meant to be shared. While I get to choose how I use it, God didn't give me it to waste. It's a gift meant to be given to help others in some way, even if that way is quite small.

This couple proved that. No glasses were needed for me to see how we can all do anything we set out to do. No challenge we face or hurdle we approach is too tough to navigate when we realize that in the moment we are in, God is by our side.

That day, God stood by these love birds. I know he made the parking lot full so that I would walk in when I did, to take a little burden off by holding the door. He helped this woman control her tremors just slightly, enough to scribble a name. He was there in each touch and each mumble. While on the outside it appeared their struggles were intense, inside I know God was the one holding them together.

I pray that one day I will reach the age that this couple was. I pray that if I get that gift, I will use it as wisely as they have, to help each other. You don't have to reach old age to savor moments. Like everything in life, each moment you breathe you get to make a choice on how you are going to live it. Stop living in a blurred daze and find clarity in who you are, where you're headed and how you are supposed to use your moments.

CHAPTER 28
Together

How do you know when your family is complete? Is it the warm feeling inside when you look around the room and see everyone piled on top of one another in a friendly game of "tackle daddy"? Is it seeing yourself in each child and knowing if you added another that your heart would literally explode because you are already loving at full capacity — and you know this world may not survive another mini-you?

For me, it was the simple reminder of the restless nights when the youngest would wake up every two or three hours. One particular week, my youngest not only decided to resurrect that nighttime ritual, twice, but he confirmed that our family is totally, utterly, complete.

Whoever coined the phrase "no one said life would be easy" was a smart cookie. But I'm going to go out on a limb and venture to say that the person who was speculating on this game called life was doing so on a good not-so-good day. Maybe someone cut them off at a red light or the movie they were dying to rent was sold out. Because if they were having a really bad day, I bet they would have adjusted their word choice to something more in line with "no one ever said that getting through each minute wouldn't be next to impossible."

I bet that writer hadn't experienced a day where they were forced to function on less than two hours of sleep and try to wrangle three kids to get ready for school.

My youngest was teething. That's probably all I need to say, and anyone who has ever parented will have a rush of memories they have suppressed that will arise from deep within. Don't let them escape. Push them back into your dark memory abyss and lock them up for good. Remember your babies by their sweet smells and squishy cheeks. I wouldn't wish memories of this level of exhaustion even upon an enemy. But, we were reminded up close and personal when our typically good sleeper turned Jekyll/Hyde on us for a few nights, wide-eyed and deep-lung screaming.

The whole family suffered. The boys shared a room, so I wasn't surprised when my oldest relocated to the couch for reprieve. My daughter woke up twice screaming from a nightmare. However, I bet the nightmare she awoke to was worse than what she woke up from. Now, I realize that our literal world wasn't crumbling but for two already exhausted parents, that night about did us in. We wanted to throw in the towel — but with this venture, there's no walking away. We were in it, together.

Together. I realize that's not a common word for many families when it comes to middle-of-the-night kid experiences — or many experiences that involve kids in general. I hadn't comprehended how together we really were and how abnormal that was until we had been blessed with the news of our pregnancy with our oldest.

I always knew my husband would be a fabulous dad. I watched him shower his niece with love years before our kids were even a glimmer in our eyes. There was no question he would be an amazing and committed husband. He always put me first and still does, no matter the occasion.

But when we were pregnant with our oldest, my husband put what I knew about him into action. He came to every doctor's appointment, even to listen to the heartbeat, determined to not miss out on the experience. During my pregnancies with our daughter and youngest son, the number of times that he wasn't able to make an appointment I could count on just one hand. He hadn't come because I'd asked him. He came because he was just as excited to be a parent as I was. He came because he cared about me, about our child, and wanted to experience as much of the pregnancy as he could. That joy he experienced as an uncle for the first time was magnified to an unprecedented level when he added the title of dad to his credentials.

You see, for all three of our children's lives, my husband has been there for us every step of the way. I have never been alone during a nighttime feeding. Every time the baby would wake, he would get them from their bed, change their diaper and deliver the sweet package to me to nurse. He'd stay up with me while I did, only so he could take the baby and rock them back to sleep.

And his involvement didn't stop there. When we get the dreaded call from school that one of the kids is sick, the pressure isn't always on me to halt my day and be "mom-to-the-rescue." He is as willing as I to swoop in and take them to the doctor. In fact, he makes it a priority to even be at well check visits for our kids because he can't wait to ensure that they have a good bill of health.

Even amidst some of his own health challenges, his family comes first. When other moms laugh in a snide way about how their husbands sleep on the couch while they cook dinner, do the dishes and get the kids to bed each night, I can't relate. Because mine is there with me — sometimes doing it all while I work late. I don't relate when other moms hold a grudge for all of the hard work they do that doesn't get noticed. Because my husband acknowledges how together, somehow, we get it all done. I'm really sorry that I don't relate. But I just don't.

This isn't meant to parade my husband around as man of the year, although to me, he totally deserves it! But I feel like it's time I stand up and share the truth, and I know I'm not alone. The only way I make it through my day is because of him. That night, when my youngest was a screaming terror, I awoke to find that my husband was already rocking him back to sleep, comforting him even though exhaustion was knocking at his door.

It's time to put a PSA out there for dads. Not all dads are careless, uninvolved or missing. Just like each of us in life, you get the choice to show up and bring your A game. We all get that choice — dads and moms alike.

My husband is proof that you don't have to live up to the expectations the world sets for you, especially when they are set low. You can be a dad that not only plays on the floor with your kids but also makes sure their teeth are brushed, and their clothes are washed. You can help with dinner and support your wife in her career. And I may take a gamble in saying this, but I bet more dads are like my husband than we let on.

I need him. How do I do it all, being a working mom of three, you may ask? One word — him. To all those dads who are in it with us, thank you for making life bearable. Thank you for holding us together and being as far in on this parenting gig as we are. Thank you for breaking the mold and ignoring any stereotypes this world has tried to impress upon you.

Thank you for being YOU. Because of you, my husband, I know nothing in life is easy, but it's possible and bearable knowing I'm not in it alone.

CHAPTER 29
I Love You, Too, Momma

I'm a socialite. Stick me in a solitary space, and I'll start talking to the wall. Many times, my mouth just won't stay closed. This can be both a blessing and a curse. A blessing when I see an injustice and stand up for it or when I get empowered presenting in front of groups of people. A blessing because it allows me to take risks. But a curse for sure, too. When I see injustice, sometimes I don't know when to back down. Or I'll take a risk before I think through if the benefits outweigh it. My verbal expressions are definitely both my ammo and my crutch.

My son has the same problem. He loves to talk, and it tends to get him in trouble. At school, he couldn't help but answer literally every question the teacher asked. That struggle happened at home, too. He would forget, like me, how to use his muscle to close his trap. I couldn't be mad at him as it's in the genes.

So, you can understand my amazement when my then 18-month-old baby girl still hadn't said a peep.

From the day she was born, she was an observer. With my oldest, I always had to cart around a slew of toys to occupy him while my daughter would sit on my lap for an hour and look around contently, smiling at everyone with whom she made eye contact.

She was my "cuddle bug;" my "relaxed princess." I loved every second of her at that age, grateful for her ability to not overwhelm us or be overwhelmed by anything. I so don't relate!

I thought it was just her disposition; she was an introvert and that she would talk when she was ready and had something brilliant to say. But I refused to be the mom who didn't take action when something needed to be addressed, so when I was nine months pregnant with her baby brother, I accepted the fact that while her sweetness was off the charts, her verbal development could use some work. I took her for a hearing screening that kicked off a multitude of tests proving that she needed speech therapy.

She started to repeat sounds and animal noises, and we got her to say more than the three or four words in her initial vocabulary. She started to articulate her wants and needs, in conjunction with key sign language words. That whole motto "It takes a village" is right, especially when it comes to helping kids reach their full potential! I felt like our speech therapist became an added member of our family, and my daughter felt so, too. Especially when therapy transitioned to taking place at her school, and she was unwilling to share her speech therapist with any of her school friends.

When she got to a point where we felt like her improvement was leveling out, we basked in the excitement of her progress but knew that she still had work to do. While we still focused on her articulation, we also worked as a family to close our mouths and to try to listen, which was especially hard for me and my oldest son. He tried to help, getting out letter books and, while reading them to her, he would have her repeat his words. If what she said wasn't perfect, he would go slower and try to help her a second time. Her growth was a family dedication. Because of it, I got to hear her sweet voice and all that came with it … the "no's" and the "mine's." The "he hurt me" and the "but I want it ..." and I wouldn't change it for the world.

A few months after we concluded her first round of speech therapy, I was taking my daughter to bed following our normal evening routine of bath, brushing teeth, and getting a drink of water. I propped her up on the side of her bed, and I talked to her, about her day and who we needed to pray for that night. I laid her down and covered her up in her polka dot blanket. I blew her a kiss and said, "I love you sweet girl." As I walked out of the room, that voice, the one that I'd prayed months before to hear, whispered back, "I love you, too, Momma."

I about fell to the floor in tears. I always knew she loved me. She gave me plenty of hugs and Eskimo kisses. We played together, and she liked to scoot her little body back until her bottom fell perfectly in my lap with a book to read. There was no question that love overflowed here in our household ... but this was the first time I had heard her say it. I knew how long of a journey it had been for us to get her to this point. The fact that she chose those words at that moment to articulate what she was feeling made me overjoyed.

This one sweet soul, who struggled to say words, put energy forth to tell me that she loves me. How many times in life do we actually put energy into something as simple as that?

When we don't hug our family or hold onto grudges for years? Or when we don't say hi to a co-worker who we walk by in the hallway, just because we're tired or don't feel like it? What about visiting someone who needs us? Our lives are too hectic; we have too many demands; we don't make time. I'm guilty of all this, too. I have the same excuses. I one-hundred percent acknowledge I am very far from sainthood.

But when I heard my daughter's affirmation of her love for me, I realized that showing love to others doesn't have to be so challenging. It's a smile. It's a simple phone call. It's saying those three words — I love you — even when they are the hardest to say, not because you can't articulate it, but because of the barriers you put up for yourself. Her barriers were real and hard. Her tongue didn't want to curl just right to say what all along she was feeling. But for us … it's easy to say, even though we chose not to.

Don't stand in your own way. Be joyous that we live in a world where we can express our feelings outwardly and do it.

Today, reach out and touch someone's life. Be the love that they need. You never know how those three words will change them, and you, in the process.

CHAPTER 30

A Garden of Love

I may have been a girl raised in the city, but my heart begs for the slow pace, fresh air and vast land only the country can bring. So, when my husband and I decided to move into our first home together, it was an easy decision to stop looking in the city and venture out into the small towns peppered a tad farther south.

I grew up with some country living in my genes as my grandparents had a farm I'd frequented nearly every weekend of my childhood. I loved so much about that farm, but their garden was among my favorites. When we found the perfect home with the perfect space to plant our own, we knew it was exactly where we were meant to be.

From tomatoes and peppers to zucchini and squash, we started out with the veggies that we were promised would survive nearly everything. Once we got comfortable and confident with those, we added in some new varieties. Beans, kale, lettuce, cucumbers and sweet potatoes. Our trick to success? Horse manure and newspaper. One to nourish the soil and one to tame the weeds. Those two pretty much do the trick. Well, those and the fence.

For every hundred things to love about living outside the city, comes a few that are not so pleasant, like bugs, rodents, critters — all of which freak me out. I'm sure city-dwellers experience these pests, too, but there is something about the country and the abundance of "wildlife" that my soul yearns for.

Deer cross our streets, so you have to always be on the lookout. Each year, just as we are getting our garden perfected, we have to pay close attention to the rabbits that seem to come in droves. In the spring, you just have to walk outside any time of the day, and you can count more rabbits than you have fingers.

The rabbits love our yard about as much as we do. They hop out of the safe-haven they have made under our deck and decide to find the perfect spot typically in the middle of the yard to deliver their litter. We've come to be pros at spotting them post-delivery. We keep watch so as to ensure the kids don't accidentally fall into one of the burrows or mistakenly touch a baby. If so, the momma won't come back typically, and we can't care for that little ball of sweetness like their mother can.

As sweet as these rabbits are, they are a welcomed addition to everywhere in my yard except one place. The garden. Eat as much grass as you want; live under the deck for as long as you desire. But please, please do not eat my home-grown veggies. I've had that talk with them and for years, they've listened. But the year we extended the garden triple its original size, I think that temptation got the best of them. They couldn't help it, and before we knew it, a mound that we thought was that of a sweet potato plant was really a bunny nest nestled right into the heart of our beautiful garden.

I'm not sure how they got in because the fence we erected was pristine. Stakes, chicken wire and all was meant to keep in what was supposed to be there and out what wasn't. Bunnies included. But all we had to see was the fur on a mound to know no good attempt would keep out our momma friend.

At first, I was livid. We had not only tripled the garden size but tripled the produce. I had plans for what was growing, and those plans didn't include rabbit food.

I did research, figuring out how to relocate a rabbit nest, and after reading all resources decided to let down my guard and accept the fact that we were in a pickle, and I don't mean one that I planned to make from my growing cucumbers. Patience, yet again, was something I had to work on because the only thing that would fix this situation was the babies growing and moving on.

We worked in the garden like our neighbors hadn't made it their home and prayed that as the bunnies took field trips, they would opt to eat the grass growing in through the fence instead of the luscious lettuce leaves. We checked the garden each day, and to our surprise, noticed no change. I stalked the garden and could even be found using a pair of the kid's binoculars to watch their behaviors.

I watched one sweet little bunny each day. She would cautiously walk around close to her nest to find some grass to nibble on. Each day, that's what she did. And as she grew, so did our garden. Our lettuce reached crazy heights, and the kale was out of control. We had volunteer tomatoes growing out of our ears. Our garden was abundant. And our bunny baby was sweet, cute and stuck.

Our fence had no gate, and while I had seen the hopping abilities of a scared momma bunny, this little baby didn't stand a chance, and if she had, there's no way she would have found her way back home. I worried and after more research realized we would have to help her by catching her and setting her free. It took me days to figure out a game plan, and one night, when the kids were tucked in bed, we ventured outside with a bucket and a pole, praying that this baby would realize we were there to help.

It was hilarious. We chased this little critter that would fit in the palm of our hand back and forth in the garden until we had put in a good workout for the day. That sweet bunny was smart. She knew where to hide where we couldn't see her and had speed like I never expected. But somehow, someway, we cornered her. I swooped in with the bucket. She was caught. And stressed.

Quickly, and without touching her with anything but a massive glove, I relocated her to the deck and slowly encouraged her to scatter under it, where I had hoped she would find her mom because moms always make things right. I had watched her defy all odds and find the safest place for her baby to grow, albeit in the middle of my garden, but that fence, that we built to keep bunnies out, actually kept her baby safe from other predators.

That night I prayed; yes, I prayed for a bunny. Because while I hate to admit it, I had become quite fond of our garden dweller. I worried, hoping that her relocation wouldn't be hard for her momma to find her so that she could continue to show her the ropes.

The next day, I went out on the deck and peered around, hoping she would take another field trip from her new dwelling and eat the semi-lush grass that desperately needed to be cut. I looked hard and nearly missed seeing her hiding in the yard. Her coat blended well, and her instincts had set in. She knew what to do to not be seen. I watched her, though, and as she got comfortable with my presence, she started to nibble and hop, making her way around the yard and back to the deck. I never saw her again after that day, but I knew that all would be well.

Even with an unwanted member in our garden, the plants survived, so much so that I canned more than 90 cans of tomatoes, pasta sauce and pickles, more than our family could eat in a year. We had sweet potatoes galore and I ate lettuce and kale salads for weeks. Our sunflowers grew tall and shaded some plants in the garden and I reaped enough beans to make a few batches of them for dinner.

The rabbits, those we had worked so hard to keep out, came in. When a feast was served on a proverbial silver platter before them, they never took more than they needed. They didn't touch what those who had helped them live wanted too much to grow. They didn't need much. A few blades of grass and maybe a radish leaf or two. They ate what was necessary and not a bit more.

I know they were just a family of rabbits and me a gardener, but when you get on your hands and knees to work the land, planting seeds and watching them grow, you become one with it and one with God. You come to respect the worms because they keep your soil loose and the bees because they help pollinate. You realize that we are all here together and each of us has a purpose.

That little bunny taught me the importance of giving all that we had worked so hard for to save the life of one. In giving up completely, I reaped more than I sowed. I gained more than I planned.

My produce was bountiful, and the bunny, alive. You see, this garden we grew, yes, it's for our family, but I have realized it's more than the produce I pick. It's a garden of love, where we take the kids to laugh together as we squish cherry tomatoes accidentally and they pick green ones when we aren't looking. It's a place where we grow and share, whether that's with co-workers, family, friends or the new bunny family that opted to move in.

This little bunny taught me that no matter the situation, in giving more you are destined to receive more. Always.

SECTION 7

THE JOURNEY

Life is a journey. While you may always be working toward something — a career advancement, a growing family or another bucket list item — once you reach where you think you ought to be, you will likely realize that there's still more to be done. You are here for a purpose. Every breath that you take is meant to fuel you for the road ahead. Every stumble is meaningful, shaping you for your next destination. All you need to do to be prepared for this journey is to make sure that who you allow to be your guide is God, the One who will lead you down the right paths.

Cherish Today

My Life. Period.

My Last Day

Get Me

Dream On

CHAPTER 31
Cherish Today

After church each Sunday, I always enjoy chatting with other parishioners. I recall a conversation I had years ago with the mother of a friend of mine, not long after my husband and I found out we were pregnant with our oldest. She and I celebrated together as we talked of the unknowns of pregnancy that were destined to come, and while some were nerve-wracking, many were thrilling. What would a kick feel like? Would I notice it? Whose features would they favor, mine or my husband's?

At that point, all I could do was daydream about this sweet soul growing each day in my belly. After a previous miscarriage, nothing mattered more to me than making sure our little baby arrived here in mint condition and doing everything I could to all but ensure that. When I say nothing else mattered, I meant it. Even my body.

My friend's mom and I laughed about the belly pooch that I had begun to sport as the pregnancy finally felt real now that others could see our miracle, too. As proud of the pooch as I was, I had to laugh about the reality that my bikini days were over. Her wise advice was to not dwell on the extra weight but rather to celebrate it. She challenged me to be happy with what I had today because tomorrow, change could happen.

She was right. I never expected to gain more than 65 pounds during my pregnancy, which was a lot to handle for this girl's 5-foot-2 frame. And imagine gaining that much and more during each of my pregnancies! But I wouldn't change it for the world. I cherish each of my babies, even if it does mean I will definitely never wear a bikini again.

My priorities have changed for sure. While I used to love makeup, making sure that my dark circles are covered doesn't always make the to-do list. That random acne that those of us in our 30s are not supposed to get? Well, I just own it. And no one has to know that sometimes I have to tuck my belly in thanks to its lack of elasticity!

I'm just happy that I have a belly and one that functions properly. I am thankful that that space occupied a few kids and despite several concerning times during each pregnancy, it blessed my life with all three.

No stretch mark will ever stand between me and my gratefulness.

When my son and I sat down to pray before bed one night, I was reminded of the conversation I had with my friend's mother many years prior when he was that sweet little bun in the oven. I always tried to teach him that prayers are meant to not just ask God for things but to use them as a direct line to thank Him for what we have. It's a tough concept for little ones, but this one night I think the concept finally registered.

We were cuddling under a blanket on our couch as we said our prayers, and when it got to the point to where we started offering up prayers of petition, he told me he wanted to thank God for the "comfy cozy," the name he decided to give the blanket. I agree that the warmth and family time the blanket provided was worth thanking God for, but I thought it was time to make sure that my son knew what other things we should be grateful for.

I shared that not everyone has a blanket, so we should be thankful that while this one is extra soft, we are lucky to have one altogether. He furrowed his eyebrows, confused, and I realized that he had never considered that some people didn't have a blanket at all. Hence, the conversation began.

We talked about our house, and how we should be thankful for having shelter each night and beds to sleep in. My son chimed in, thankful for food, too. I shared that not everyone gets to choose from so many food options each day, and some don't even know the next time that they will get to eat.

Our prayers evolved to talk about the people in our lives. I explained how lucky he was to have a momma and a daddy, and that not everyone has both. It was too deep of a topic, but after I said it, I could tell he immediately understood. He had a moment of sadness but acknowledged that their mommas and daddies were in heaven waiting for those they love. He then thanked God for us.

As we cuddled closer, we talked about how grateful we should be for our legs, our hands and our eyes. Not everyone has those, and we should even be thankful for our hair as I explained to him that some people lose their hair when they are sick.

And as our prayers came to a close, I gave him a kiss that he tried to wipe off, and before he walked to his room, I told him that we should all be thankful for what we have today. I definitely made sure that he knew that he is one of my special things I am most thankful for.

That sweet boy was the one in my belly when I had that conversation with my friend's mom. He started the downhill spiral of the stomach I once had, yet in praying with him that night, I realized how grateful I am for all that I did have. Today I have hands that can write and legs that can take me places. I have eyes to see each of their sweet smiles and arms to wrap around them. I get to cuddle under the "comfy cozy" and share elephant kisses because those can't be wiped off.

But thankfulness should go beyond what you can see and into what you can feel. I woke up this morning. I took a breath. But if tomorrow I couldn't do that, I'd be thankful for the love I feel deep within. That can never be taken from me.

My friend's mom was right. We should be thankful for what we have today because everything could change tomorrow. But what she didn't tell me was that while things may change, and they always will, tomorrow I will have time to love a little more, to dream a little bigger, and to share more happiness with those around me.

Who cares about wrinkles? They just mean you've lived. Who cares about stretch marks? They mean you've experienced a love deeper than you thought possible. Those dark circles may show your restless nights of worry and concern, but you had someone to worry about who was worth more to you than even yourself.

Don't hide behind these things because they aren't what matter most. For each are merely visible roadmaps of your life as you journey through it. Tomorrow, you may be different than you are today, that's promised, but you are here. For that, find gratitude. For we are all here for a brief time. Let go of your earthly concerns and cherish today. Cherish this very moment.

CHAPTER 32

My Life. Period.

One night he started singing it. My husband quickly got my attention before my son noticed we were listening and decided to protest any further exercising of his vocal cords. But he didn't; in fact, when I started belting out the lyrics with him, he got more excited, surprised that I, too, knew a rendition of the "Baby Shark" song.

When I asked him where he had learned that song, he shied away as if it was a secret. That was until I started chiming in. Music class, for him! But for me, I was taught it sitting on a tree stump in the middle of the wilderness far away at 4H camp.

"Baby Shark," such a fun song, brings back memories for me of independence and childhood wonder but also embarrassment and fear.

I was 12 when I attended camp. It was my first real trip away from my parents, and while most other kids who boarded the bus to head into a bug-filled, parent-free zone were filled with excitement, I felt a tinge of nervousness, stressed about how my body would react in an environment that I could no longer control.

Being 12 wasn't so easy for me. Outside of the awkwardness associated with every kid that age, my body had deemed it time for me to undergo puberty. What every girl is anxious for happened, and when it happened to me, it didn't stop.

My mom and I had never talked about it until the day it showed up. While for most, life gets back to normal after a week, for me, it took more than a year. You see, once my body decided it was time to introduce me to "Aunt Flo," I learned that my body wasn't built like most. My mom was determined to only share what my innocent mind could understand and prayed along the way that I did not inherit our family's medical issue. While her prayers were heard, the outcome wasn't what we had hoped.

I bled. And bled and bled. And it didn't stop. No matter what I did or how I moved, it happened. My time of the month was all the time, which was hard to face at that age.

After several attempts at treating the symptoms, the gynecologist determined it was time to come face-to-face with the culprit. I made my way to my regular check-up, thinking I was going to have another verbal meeting with my doctor until they handed me a gown and asked me to remove all my clothing. My mom looked panicked, and I'm sure I had the same look on my face, too, as I hadn't a clue what was in store for me. I'm glad I didn't. Because when the tools came out, and the exam began, I screamed a scream so loud that I'm sure the entire floor could hear.

While I inherited her deep brown eyes, I also inherited her uterus, one filled with tissue scarring that leads to painful and ongoing periods. What had taken my mom's ability to have more kids away many years ago through a hysterectomy proved that it would never leave our family, just skip to the next generation to torment. This innocent 12-year-old drew the short end of the stick.

That year got harder before it got easier. I remember getting excited about the upcoming school mixer. My mom drove a friend and me, but once we arrived, my friend got out of the car, and when I went to stand up, I had to sit back down. I had ruined the car seat, just by sitting. I watched my friend go inside as mom and I inched the car farther away.

We hadn't even had our "family life" class in school before family life hit so close to home. So, when we did, I was hopeful to learn more about my disorder, but instead, I left terrified. I realize now how critical this class is for the majority of my classmates, but it left me confused. I remember a teacher talking about birth control and how our religion did not support the use of any artificial measures, including the pill; the pill that I took.

I didn't realize that what I was taking was that pill; a pill that others used to prevent life was the pill that I was using to save mine.

I went home that night in tears, telling my mom that God was mad at me for taking the only medication we could find that could help me live semi-normal. She hugged me, cried, too, and told me that God loved me no matter what.

That year I went to 4H camp. I was nervous about whether I had packed enough feminine products, if anyone would question my medication and if my period would cease long enough for me to enjoy the week.

There were times it did because I have lots of awesome memories such as learning how to shoot a gun and enjoying the simplicity of life on a canoe. I learned how to conquer my fears by going zip lining and asking a boy to dance after dinner one evening. But my period never left, and what I feared would happen did. My bleeding came with a vengeance and didn't cease. I made friends with the counselors who worked in the medical hut as they monitored me. We called my mom, and while she was ready to come and get me at a moment's notice, I told her I wanted to try to make it.

My group leader took care of me, never questioning if she needed to take me back to the room to change. When everyone else went swimming, she and I would go have fun somewhere else.

She let me live how I needed to, and because of their kindness, I had an experience of a lifetime filled with lots of memories, including the "Baby Shark" song I still sing to this day.

When my son and I sang each word of the song together, it made me teary-eyed. When I was diagnosed with my disorder, I learned that having kids may have not been in my future. As I sang the song and even did the hand motions to go with it, I felt at peace. Not only did my body get whipped into shape, it did so enough for me to have three beautiful babies, making my life so much sweeter than I could have imagined.

I'm not sure if any of the kids in my 7th grade class ever knew what was going on. Maybe no one noticed, or some did but just looked the other way. Or maybe they were just kids and loved me nonetheless.

There are pieces of each of us that we opt to hold close, not letting others peek in and see. Some of us judge others, generalizing what we think is going on when we really don't know. This 12-year-old girl at the gynecologist received lots of stares and judgment, let me tell you.

You never know another person's internal battle. The person who checked you out at the grocery who didn't smile may have gotten some bad news before work, and she is just trying to make it through her shift. Or the waiter who took forever to fulfill your order may be taking more tables to try to pad his paycheck to cover an unexpected expense. Or the little kid sitting next to the pool with her feet dangling in the water may not be scared to swim, but can't that day for a reason she can't control.

Don't be a critic. Leave those judging eyes at home and replace them with ones filled with kindness.

Smile at others, and when you do really look at them, letting them know that you see them for who they are and where they are, and that life is going to be okay. As you walk away, pray that whatever burden they are carrying, God is helping to carry it with them. I'm confident that someone did that for me. Somewhere along my journey, someone took a moment to ask God to let me get through it and see the other side. He listened. He always does. And just like the "Baby Shark" song ends with a happy shark, so am I, safe at last.

CHAPTER 33

My Last Day

I'm confident there is a reason that God placed in each of us the ability to not dwell on the inevitable, the fact that there will be a day that will be our last. At least our last here. To live means we must push out of our thoughts the reality that our day will come, hopefully, later than sooner, when our families will grieve for their loss. But on that day, their loss is our gain ... if you believe.

There are some times in life, though, when we do ponder exactly what this day will be like. When we visit an ailing family member or attend the visitation of a loved one, who is no longer with us. We allow ourselves a brief moment to consider what that will be like for us, and then we compartmentalize the fact that there was a day that they, too, once ignored the unavoidable.

Sometimes I open that closed off part of my thoughts to that destined reality, although most times not in a serious manner. I mean, if I had to choose my last supper, I'd opt for homemade sweet potato fries with a pairing of sautéed kale accompanied with a dash of olive oil and fresh crispy garlic.

If I knew today would be my last day, after eating my last supper, I'd visit Cave Hill Cemetery, one of the most popular in the city as it is the resting place of many notable individuals. KFC's Colonel Sanders has a space nestled somewhere in the nearly 300 acres of beauty. The locals all look for Harry Collins's grave site, as he was one of Louisville's most popular magicians in his time. Years ago, on my birthday, my husband and I spent the morning doing whatever I wished, but with the goal to find Patty Hill's headstone, as she was the woman who came up with the "Happy Birthday" song.

We never found her, but we did bring a stale loaf of bread, and we did what I do every time I come, and if it were my last day, I'd do it as well. Feed the abundance of ducks. After I tossed my last piece of bread, I would find a clear spot in the grass and lie down, savoring the warmth of the sun on my face. Even though I'd never get to look at them again, I'd bring my camera and take pictures of the headstones.

That's what makes me happiest; the simplicity of it all where I can visibly see God's beauty everywhere in a sea of silence.

There is a peace I feel when I visit a cemetery. Maybe it's the fact that God is ever-most present. While I allow myself to open the thoughts around my fate, I do put away the fact that six feet under are vessels of many souls before me. That's a tad creepy, if I do say so myself. But I think it's healthy to allow yourself, from time to time, the chance to press the pause button on life and realize that if you're always in the fast lane, you will miss everything that this life is supposed to be.

My kids help me pause most days whether I want to or not. Their endless questions and wanting of playmates have pulled me away from the dishes and my thoughts to be in the moment with them. That's of course when

I allow myself to. But when I do, I always feel the need to hug them a little tighter and request lots of kisses, because I know that there will be a day where that simple gesture may be non-existent.

That day might be soon because nowadays when I ask for kisses before bed, all three shake their heads. My oldest affirmed that kisses are yucky, and he wiped them off. I kissed him anyway and told him to be thankful for my kisses because there may be a day that I won't be there to give them to him.

Oops … don't make the mistakes that I do. Why on earth would I say something like that to a kid? I quickly noted that I'll always be there so no need to worry about that. But he did look up at me and say, "You won't be able to kiss me, Momma, because you'll be in heaven?" "Yes, sweet boy, that's where I hope to be. But I promise I'll always be here to give you kisses." So, I gave him another, and he rubbed it off but told me he was rubbing it in.

Now I understand how hard it is to be a parent, watching your children evolve from being embarrassed about kisses to having to have heavy chit-chats. My dad and I have those — our "deep conversations," I call them — and one day our chat evolved to talk about the topic none of us can escape. As an only child, my parents occasionally drop little hints of what they want during their funerals. This day was a continuation of that.

We've talked about preferred songs and even clothes that he wants to be buried in. In fact, he is determined that he will be buried in blue jeans and be lowered into the earth while blasting the rock-n-roll beat of Kansas's "Carry On Wayward Son."

But this one chat with my dad was about caskets and how he wants a simple pine box. Nothing fancy. I begged him to write this all down or even to pre-arrange his wants so that when I am left to grieve and try to pick up the pieces, I'm not playing an internal battle with myself of wanting to give him what he deserves but rather what he wants. Nah, he said, you're a big girl. You'll know what to do. Then I teared up, and that was all of that conversation I could have. That little wiggle room I allowed to talk about such difficult topics was gone, and we went back to talking about other subjects that made me smile. The death topic was pushed back into the box hidden deep within until the next time I realize the inevitable doesn't go away.

But it does get easier. The more I randomly blurt out things to my kids makes me realize that the end isn't really the end. My oldest talks a lot about heaven, and how when we both are there how much fun we will have. Yes, my son, we totally will. But until then we have the now, and that's pretty fun, too.

Until then, we must live our dash. While I do enjoy the uniqueness of each headstone I observe when visiting the cemetery, I realize each only gives a little glimpse of the person it represents, leaving much about that person's life to one's imagination. Sure, you learn their "years" — their birth year and the year they took their last breath — but who were they in that time in between? How did they live their dash?

One day, our day will come; it's one of the two constants we all will face. The two dates on our headstones are just that — dates that are out of our control. We all were born, and one day, we all will be born again, hopefully into some place much better than where we are today. But until then, what's most important in life is how we live in the now. Some of us may show up in a beautiful package and others may cross that finish line battered and bruised. No matter how we arrive, what matters is that we have truly lived every ounce of that dash.

What would you do if you knew today was your last? Who would you hug once more or apologize to? What meal would you indulge in and what beauty of this world would you capture? Where would you want to take your last breath and with whom would you want to share it?

Maybe we should spend more time talking about what's to come so that we realize how precious this moment is. The time we get living our dash is the time we get to leave our legacy. Make today count, because you never know when it will be your last.

CHAPTER 34
Get Me

As a kid, I spent time doing things that weren't typical "girl" stereotypes. I liked going fishing with my dad. There it was quiet, and while my dad cast the line (because I would take out an eye doing so), I found myself playing with the basket of crickets. Those spiny creepy crawlies were doomed, but I made friends with a few and would secretly lead them to safety when dad's gaze was fixed on the lake.

Most weekends in middle-school, my dad and I would go to my grand-parent's farm, and I'd live in the treehouse that still had blood stains from when my dad built it. The treehouse overlooked the creek that separated us from the rest of civilization, and I would go wading in it to find crawdads.

As I grew up, I grew out of some of that childhood fun. Nowadays, if I see a cricket in the garage, I run in the opposite direction, and wading in the creek, while fun, in theory, comes with the opportunity to cut your toe on sharp rocks.

Growing up can rob you of your naiveté, but it didn't rob me of every-thing. I may have turned in my fishing pole, but I took on new adventures with my dad. Wading in the creeks didn't sound like much fun anymore but rafting on them … I was up for that!

It didn't matter that I barely met the weight requirements, turning 12 justified that I was ready for a whitewater rafting adventure. Or at least my dad said it did and I believed him. Plus, my grandma loved to raft and would be joining us; so, if Grandma could do it, have no fear, I'd make it out alive.

Gulp.

The drive there gave me plenty of time to develop a strange sensation in the pit of my stomach that I chalked up to excitement. While that feeling grew after watching the safety video, there was no option of backing out. Even river flooding and fast waters weren't going to stop this youngin' from the adventure of a lifetime.

I was set. Life jacket secured tight and helmet fastened. You could barely see me peeking through all the safety gear that was meant to help me if I got washed overboard. The flooding caused the river to move at lightning speeds, and our guide reiterated that if an accident occurred, we must stay in the middle of the river. DO NOT DRIFT TO THE BANKS. There, the river pressure would snap a little body around a tree, and there would be no going back.

Gulp again.

They positioned me in the safest spot on the raft … the very back. My grandma and I wedged our toes as far as we could in the back two spots next to the guide, knowing that he wasn't going to let a child, or a grandma, not enjoy their time. I scooted as far out on side of the raft as my nerves would allow, and when the raft hit the water, grabbed my paddle like I knew what I was doing.

While river flooding didn't allow for the typical rapid experience, we enjoyed some smaller waves, learning as a team how to dig deep to maneuver the raft. It didn't take long to know that our guide had ventured these waters regularly and if we trusted his commands, we'd navigate through as safe as possible.

Before long, besides my constant worry about what do to when I needed to go to the bathroom in the middle of a river where bathroom breaks weren't an option, I was set until we came up to the waves.

What had originally been a larger rapid had evolved into massive waves due to the flooding, and as a team, we were about to figure out if our navigation skills had been perfected. Our guide prepared us to dig in when he yelled the cue and then whispered to my grandma and me to scoot in. I followed directions, scooted closer in, wedged my feet in deeper and looked everywhere to find something to hold onto. But to no avail.

He was right. This rapid was a beast. The waves were high. The water was fast. My heart was pounding so loud I'm not sure I even heard when the waves would break. But we rode them as best as we could. We thought we were doing well until we saw a massive wave that was promised to break at the same time as we were going to ride it. There was nothing we could do. The wave was going to engulf our raft. A last-minute "hold on" from our guide prepared most, but this lightweight had no hope. I was a goner.

As the rest of the rafters recovered from getting drenched, I was trying to remember everything that the safety video had warned me about as I bobbed up and down in the water gasping for breaths. The water was so fast, taking me farther and farther away from the raft. All I could think about was doing everything possible to not become one with the trees, literally. Yet I found out quickly, within seconds, that if that was my fate, there wasn't anything I could do about it.

All I could do was yell, so yell I did. The little breath I could find in between gulps of water I used to scream "GET ME!" It felt like eternity, and I came to grips with the fact they couldn't hear me over the crashing waves until I saw a rescue bag floating within arm's reach and being held on the other end by the guide. I grabbed it, and as the guide pulled me to safety, I noticed another man on the raft pulling my dad in from the water as well.

My spot on the raft never looked so good after experiencing the river in the way that I had. The day was young and giving up wasn't an option even though I begged for it to be. The river had not only soaked me, but it washed away any false appearance of bravery. I was a scared little girl on a path of no return. There was an end, but it definitely wasn't in sight, and we had the rest of the day to hopefully get to it.

We did. We lived to tell the tale. After we made it to land, we thanked God that we made it through in one piece. As I allowed my heart to remember its normal pace, I realized that the river was everything it promised to be. A rush? I had never experienced an adrenaline blast like that. An adventure? I would say that's an understatement as it topped any experience I'd had before. Memorable? Undoubtedly.

After years of recounting this story of having a "near death" experience, I appreciate that my time on that river taught me more than I bargained for.

That day, I had to learn to trust blindly. As we became one with the water, all of us on the raft were in uncharted territory. The only person who knew the way was our guide, and he was the only person who was able to lead us to safety.

He taught us skills along the way. He helped us learn the importance of teamwork, which was critical to ensuring we maneuvered the raft around any troubled areas we could avoid. But, as with life, not every hurdle was avoidable. On days that you have to tackle one head-on, sometimes the only thing you can do is yell for help and pray that a rope will be tossed your way. Or your dad will jump out to save you, which I learned later is how my dad found his way outside the raft.

We bought the video of our crazy adventure to document the occasion. It doesn't show my wash overboard, but when dubbed to some pretty rad music it paints a memory filled with more smiles than tears. I have several more just like it. You see, that experience was "memorable," but it shaped me to take risks. Some risks you may falter on and others may wash you away altogether. But through each, you grow.

The same is true for life. In fact, life is like a river filled with a series of rapids. Sometimes you'll get to tackle rapids and other times you'll have fun surfing them. There will be flooding that will occur, and during those times, all you can do is pray to make it through in one piece. You will have times that will be fast-paced, and other quiet moments that will leave you to ponder. A lot is unknown, and no matter how many times you navigate it, new challenges will always show up.

Once you start, there's no turning back, but you can absolutely beg for help. Even when you're bobbing up and down, gasping for air in between gulps of water … just when you think that you're sinking instead of swimming, you'll have a rope within arm's reach once you open your eyes to see it. And you'll have people willing to go to any measure to pull you back in.

You can be prepared though if you're up for looking for guidance. It requires a little trust and a whole lot of faith.

No, you won't find a safety video, but one book will fill you with everything you need to make it through. The life vest may not be visible, but I promise you that He didn't throw you into this world without wrapping His arms around your chest to help you come up for air each time you need it. His life vest isn't one you remove. His rope isn't ever far from reach. With a little trust, your Guide will get you through, and if you ever have a moment of uncertainty, just find your voice deep within and scream "GET ME!" He always answers your prayers, and I promise He won't let you drift to the banks.

CHAPTER 35
Dream On

When people look at me, I'm sure they see me differently from how I see myself. Maybe to them I look put together, but inside my sanity is held by a string. Or they notice the baby weight that I have shed after carrying three kids, but it's sometimes a struggle for me to see past my stretch marks. They probably are sure that I am always a glass-half-full kind of girl when in true honesty I have talks with myself to pull my mind away from teetering on the brink of diving into negativity.

Things aren't always what they seem. I bet if I told you that instead of always listening to nursery rhymes if I get to control the radio, I would opt for a little rock-n-roll, many would be surprised. Unless you knew that my dad and I share a love for a good ol' REO Speedwagon or Kansas song. Or if you've ever played me in a game of Rock Band, you know that I can nail the lyrics to "Dream On," thanks to an early dose of Aerosmith in my blood.

Yes, if I were to write the lyrics to my life's song, it would have that constant drum beat and an intense electric guitar front and center. I would scream at the top of my lungs, just like Steven Tyler does, but I'd be begging to actually hit a high note. I would close my eyes to feel the music echo in my soul.

Each time I would climb into my dad's blue Toyota pick-up truck, he taught me the power of music, whether it was intentional or not. Some of my earliest memories took place strapped on top of the arm console, positioned as close to him as was feasibly possible, jamming as we traveled from point A to point B.

This was where my dad fed me his love for rock-n-roll and planted the seed for mine. He would put in his cassette tapes of Guns-n-Roses and Tom Petty, and we would belt out the lyrics while he would unexpectedly grab my leg to play guitar on it during the solos. I'm not sure how we made it without him having a plethora of tickets on his record, but somehow, we did and were energized by the time we reached our destination.

I couldn't have been much older than 10 when I went to my first concert with my dad. Of course, we saw the one and only Aerosmith. It didn't matter that we were in the nose-bleed section because I was there with Dad and together we were jamming! That's what meant the most.

Even my wedding wouldn't be complete without our band. Our daddy-daughter dance wasn't destined to be one filled with tears. Instead, we laughed as we belted out Aerosmith's "I Don't Want to Miss a Thing." Tears were still there, as beneath the hard exterior my dad tries to portray lives a sensitive soul who wants nothing more than to see his little girl fly. And fly, Daddy, I am doing.

I may not always know the direction, but I'm flying or attempting to. What my dad doesn't know is that throughout my childhood, each song we sang together became etched lyrics in my soul, paving the way for me to not only fly but to attempt to soar.

In the rusted truck, I learned that life wasn't going to be easy, but it would be important to "take it easy." No, that doesn't mean to just roll with the punches and let life happen to you, but rather find a place to "make your stand" and then breathe. The Eagles were right.

He taught me that no matter where I go, I should never feel like I'm going there alone. Even if it seems like no one is there, you've always got God, and the direct line to him by offering up a prayer.

Don't just offer one up, live on it! Realize that you may not have everything you want, but God will give you everything you need. Bon Jovi knew that it's important to "hold on to what we've got" and honestly, it doesn't matter if you've made it big. What matters is that "we have each other."

Life is a series of moments all strung together as you make your way through your journey. That's where the fun happens, and the memories are made. Hold on to those moments and if you can, find a way to "stay lost in them forever." Steven Tyler knew the importance of those times, and I agree when I shout it from the rooftops that every moment spent with those I love is "a moment I treasure."

But the road won't be easy. Sometimes you will take on the world, and rock it, just like Queen tells you to. Other times you will find that you'll continue to pick up where you left off, and you are "on the road again" not sure where you are heading, hopeful to just keep "turning the pages." But "don't stop believing." Always "hold on to that feeling." And know that any time of year, you can always find your way back home. Just like our heavenly home, no matter how many times you check out, you can never leave. A piece of your heart will always be there.

In fact, sometimes it's the difficulties that help you navigate through this life and lead you down the direction you need to head.

Only when you reach your final destination will you be able to find true peace. My sweet wayward son, only when you're done will you be able to "lay your weary head to rest." Kansas was right. "Don't you cry no more," surely heaven waits for you.

As I write my life's song, I think Sheryl Crow would sing my lyrics, and maybe the core theme would be in line with Nirvana's "Come as You Are." I may occasionally add in a saxophone like Bob Seger did in "Turn the Page" but I would definitely have several guitar solos like a good ol' Lynyrd Skynyrd concert would. You would snap your fingers and shuffle your feet to the catchy tune like Manfred Mann's "Doo Wah Diddy Diddy." I would make sure that I'd have an Aerosmith-inspired microphone stand filled with flair and memories from along the way.

Write your song. Sing it from the rooftops. Promise me that you will "dream until your dreams come true."

CONCLUSION

YOUR CHOICE

The difference between living an ordinary life and an extraordinary one is the one extra choice you make. The key here is that YOU get to make that choice. Yet, having a guide to help you in that process is critical, especially because life isn't easy, even on our easiest of days.

So how do you make that choice each day, each minute, each moment? As I have reflected on my life's experiences thus far, filled with both challenging situations and seemingly mundane moments, I've found that the secrets to harnessing true perspective are:

- **A realization that you were never meant to traverse your life's unknown alone.** Find your spiritual anchor — such as a belief in God — as it will help you to see that you are a part of a magnificent and interwoven world where we all have value, can create value for others and are meant to live lives of meaning and worth.
- **A persistent belief that extraordinary moments were never meant to come with fireworks.** While it would be ideal for them to be identified more easily, most stem from mundane and seemingly ordinary interactions. Be open to those moments, for they have the power to shape your perspective even more than you could expect.

- **An understanding that perfection isn't attainable, but it was never meant to be.** Your perfection and His perfection aren't synonymous, and once you accept that, you can find peace not only with those around you, but within yourself as well.
- **A willingness to intentionally pause, soak in the moments and see the good that's around you.** It's baked in our experiences — both the joyous memories and the challenging occasions. It's woven into the DNA of others we meet, even if for a brief time. When you live your life this way, you'll find that you have allowed yourself the freedom to choose what your life will be shaped by.
- **A belief that one person, YOU, has the power to make an impact, to make a difference and to leave a legacy.** Never underestimate what one person, one interaction or one action can do in the life of another for it all started with One, and one has the power to change everything.
- **A conscious effort to not just see the good but to *be* the good, and at the core of that is living your life with love as your guide.** Choose to love. Choose to forgive. Choose to believe. This doesn't come as second nature to most, but the easy road isn't always the one that leads to fulfillment. And remember, when making these choices, they don't just apply to how you see others, but also how you see yourself. Love yourself. Forgive yourself. Believe in yourself.
- **A dedication to never let the journey hinder you, but rather propel you.** Life is filled with twists and turns, highs and lows, joys and sorrows. Seek to always have faith that the trials and traumas you experience don't have to make you weak, but can strengthen you in ways that may currently be unfathomable. While your life's journey is full of unpredictability, never lose sight of your end destination and believe that every hill, every twist and every hurdle you face may help you find deeper purpose.

NOW, THE CHOICE IS UP TO YOU ...

Much in your life is out of your control, so to live a life in perspective, you must control the only thing that is within your grasp: YOU.

YOU get to choose how YOU react to the cards life deals you. YOU get to choose how YOU see the things in your life happen to you or happen for you. YOU get to choose your dreams and the energy YOU invest in them. YOU get to choose YOU.

While challenges are promised to arise, when you choose to live a life in perspective, you will come to see that in your brightest of days and darkest of nights, He is always with you. YOU can choose to always have faith.

I understand this is easier said than done, but having faith means so much more when you've been on the brink of not having it. Believe with your entire being that you are a part of a larger plan, one that is destined for goodness. Most of what you face will never make sense to you, but if YOU have faith, you know that every challenge endured is an opportunity to allow the roots He has placed in you to deepen.

YOU. Above all else, believe in YOU because He does. Know that nothing is ever perfect, and yet it all always is, including YOU. Life may not go as planned, but just because to you, it's not perfection, know that to God everything is. He made YOU. Everything He touches is designed the way He intended it to be. Perfection is out of your grasp, but perfect imperfection isn't. When you make mistakes or find yourself broken, know that the journey is meant to shape YOU. Let it.

YOU have the power. YOU have the ability. YOU are capable of more than you know. When life seems so overwhelming, I find myself questioning how me, one little blip in the universe, is worth it. But take a look around. It all starts with one. One flower with the strength to bloom lays the seeds for others to join it. One bright star drew many to celebrate the birth of our Savior. One act of kindness has the ability to create a ripple effect of positivity. One person, YOU, has the power to change the world and make a difference. But it all starts with changing YOU first.

This challenge I have for you is easier than it seems, yet more gratifying than expected.

When YOU live a life of perspective, you allow yourself to live every single moment purposefully. You are driven by having faith, wavering as it may be, but built on a trust that God is with you.

When you choose perspective, you choose imperfection and embrace the fact that perfect imperfection is more beautiful than perfection ever could be. You own YOU, knowing that YOU, your words, your actions and your reactions are the only facets of this existence that YOU can control. Through that, YOU make the conscious choice to harness the moment and fully live.

YOU have the choice, right now. YOU have the choice when you wake up tomorrow. YOU are given the choice when life goes beautifully and when hiccups occur. The choice is always there, and the only one who can choose it is YOU.

YOU get to choose the lens through which YOU view life. Choose wisely. Choose to *color today pretty*.

ACKNOWLEDGMENTS

Our lives are filled with walking angels, meant to guide you when you fall off your path; meant to build your confidence when you live in self-doubt; and meant to prove to you that anything is possible if you believe in it. I have had the opportunity to meet many of these very people as they have believed in me when I questioned my purpose. They encouraged me to find my voice even when it was potentially robbed from me. They held me together when I felt myself falling apart.

Thank you. Thank you for helping me realize my story is one worthy of being shared.

Thank you to my family for letting me share our stories. I am grateful for your continued support as I navigate the path God has paved for me. And speaking of Him, I am grateful that He is my glue, always guiding me even amidst my challenges while bestowing unexpected blessings.

To my mom, Debbie, and dad, Ty, thank you for shaping my life as one instilled in faith while always encouraging me to soar.

To my husband, Cory, thank you for loving every ounce of me and seeing my abilities even when I can't.

To my children, Eli, Lyndi and Luke, thank you for blessing me with more teachings than I could ever teach you.

To those who have given a piece of themselves as I pieced together this book that I felt called to create, thank you.

To my friends, Cathy Fyock, for providing the constructive guidance I needed to share my story; Eric Walker, for his continued belief that my story was worthy enough; and Marie Cirelli Thornsberry, for a friendship that anyone would be lucky enough to find in their lifetime.

To my editorial board filled with dedicated "Stephanie supporters" whose feedback challenged me to dig deeper than I thought feasible. Thank you Alana Baker, Julie Brickner, Cathy Fyock, Shawn Kramer and Eric Walker for being the first to peer into these messages and deem them important to share.

To the Silver Tree Publishing team for helping this book reach its full potential. Kate Colbert, Hilary Jastram and Courtney Hudson, I appreciate you sharing your expertise and wisdom with me as together we took what was once a dream and turned it into a reality.

To those who felt so strongly about this book's message that they were willing to provide a testimony to encourage others to delve into each of the book's pages. Thank you for your authenticity.

To my *Color Today Pretty* launch team who believed in the value of this book's message and helped ensure it made its way into the hands of people who needed it. Thank you for helping spread the word.

To every person who supported my dream. From coordinating fundraisers, purchasing custom wreath orders and providing personal expertise to support my promotional efforts, each of you has shown me how God has the power to work through the lives of others. Your support has given me the ammunition to never give up on a message that needs to be delivered.

There are not enough pages in a book to show my immense gratitude to each and every person whom I have met on my journey who has believed in me, supported me and pushed me to do more and to be more. All I can say is thank you. Two words with more meaning than I have the ability to express. Let it never be forgotten how one person can make a difference. Because of each of you, I have proven to myself that dreams really do come true.

ABOUT THE AUTHOR

Stephanie Feger is a passionate communicator who believes that a shift in perspective can help people live truly fulfilling lives. After working in the public relations and marketing industry for nearly 15 years, she learned that happiness isn't found in what society deems important and felt a calling to do something different. That's when she began to nurture her entrepreneurial spirit and build a brand intended to help others live to their fullest potential.

Stephanie has embraced listening to God on her journey and empowers others to join her through *Color Today Pretty*. From being a professional speaker, avid blogger and home décor business owner, Stephanie connects her passion for embracing creativity with her devotion to faith in everything she does.

Stephanie lives in a small city on the outskirts of Louisville, Kentucky, with her husband, Cory, and their three kids, Eli, Lyndi and Luke. She is a member of her community's Catholic Church and credits her personal faith for helping her overcome obstacles in life. When she isn't creating or spending time with her beloved kids, she can be found in her backyard gardening.

Learn more at www.colortodaypretty.com.

LEARN MORE

Before you close this book, open your mind to more ways to *Color Today Pretty* in your own life. **It's YOUR turn.**

You've read these pages. You've absorbed these messages. Now YOU hold the power to impact another. Remember, it starts with one. How will you use the messages sprinkled throughout to extend into your life and the lives of others you come in contact with? The opportunities are endless, but do you mind if I leave you with a challenge?

Will you help me color today pretty? My challenge to you is to start today, this very moment. Start with a smile to someone you don't know who looks as though they could use a reminder that happiness can be found. Give a hug to a loved one, for the power of human connection is immense. Write a thank you note to someone who made your day. Let someone go ahead of you in line at the grocery store or pause to let another car out at an intersection.

Start small, but know that each act of kindness has the power to have a ripple effect. In doing good for others, you will also find that the ripple effect inches its way into your heart, chiseling any callouses you once had away. In fact, I need your help to ensure that this ripple effect makes the difference it is meant to make. Each time you find yourself or someone else around you choosing to color today pretty, snap a picture of it. Write about it. Post it to social media using the hashtag #colortodaypretty. Let's show the world that we get the choice to do good, and we choose it daily! I believe that with your help, our world will not just be colored pretty, it will be downright beautiful.

Thanks to you, the charge I was given by a little boy in my dream is possible. I know that with each crayon scribble, each paint stroke and each pen line we are working together to make the world a better place.

MEET, WORK WITH AND BE INSPIRED BY STEPHANIE ...

If the messages in this book touched your heart, don't stop here. Allow Stephanie Feger of *Color Today Pretty* to continue to provide you the inspiration you need as your traverse your life's journey. Stephanie is passionate about perspective, believing that through inspiration comes transformation, and with a dash of creative therapy in the mix, you have a recipe for fulfillment.

Stephanie would love the opportunity to work with you to bring the messages of *Color Today Pretty* to you and any group — corporate or social — and help you explore them more deeply. Living a life in perspective has benefits for everyone. Personally or professionally, Stephanie is ready to help you pause the noise and savor the moments. Stephanie is excited to help others live out their life's mission with purpose and perspective. Hire her for:

- Experiential workshops
- Retreats
- Speaking engagements and keynotes
- One-on-one coaching and consultation.

To learn more about Stephanie's suite of *Color Today Pretty* offerings or to schedule her to come and engage with your group, visit **www.colortodaypretty.com**.

Made in the USA
Lexington, KY
18 June 2018